When Heaven Touches Earth

. . . .

A Little Book of Miracles, Marvels, and Wonders

with Stories from
James Van Praagh,
Sunny Dawn Johnston,
Lisa McCourt,
and More

Hier◯phantpublishing

Cover design by Emma Smith
Cover art by unchalee_foto and LilKar | Shutterstock

Hierophant Publishing
8301 Broadway, Suite 219
San Antonio, TX 78209
888-800-4240
www.hierophantpublishing.com

If you are unable to order this book from your local bookseller,
you may order directly from the publisher.

Library of Congress Control Number available upon request.

ISBN for the paper back edition: 978-1-938289-55-2
ISBN for the hardcover edition: 978-1-938289-68-2

10 9 8 7 6 5 4 3 2 1
Printed on acid-free paper in Canada

Contents

Introduction

Lisa McCourt

Is the universe a friendly place? Albert Einstein has famously claimed that this is the most important question you can ask yourself. He knew your answer to that question would determine the quality of your life. He knew the extent to which we believe the universe is a friendly place is the precise extent to which we experience joy, peace, and contentment. Conversely, if you believe the universe is a hostile place, your experience of life will bear out that belief. Science has since come a long way in validating Dr. Einstein's bang-on claim. Thanks to advances in quantum physics, we now know with verifiable scientific certainty that our beliefs affect our experience of reality.

Maybe it's not easy for you to acknowledge that up until this very moment you've been creating your reality, step by step, unwittingly, from the springboard of your individual belief system. It's likely you've never been made aware of this process, and likely you aren't even readily aware of most of your beliefs. But isn't it a relief to realize that you can change anything in your experience simply by changing your beliefs around it? This truth isn't limited to the question of whether or not the universe is friendly but extends to the very laws that govern that universe.

This book is for people who choose to believe in a force of love so immense, so all encompassing, so inextricably interwoven within everyone and everything that it transcends paltry life/death delineations.

But it's not for us believers alone. It's also for the "cuspers"—those on the cusp of believing in such a glorious and impervious force of love but who can't quite wrap their heads around it. And even though we die-hard believers cherish the accounts in this book (because we get teased a lot and enjoy validation!), the cuspers will appreciate them even more.

It's the cuspers who'll feel the quickening in their gut as they absorb these words. They're the ones who'll have the giddy, coming-home sensation wash over them as the niggling suspicions they've long buried come bubbling up to the surface of their awareness. They're the ones who will feel the chills of "Aha!" and the tingles of "Yes! Deep down, I've always known!"

Maybe you're not sure you're ready for that kind of full-on acceptance. We present-day humans like to look smart and feel in control. We like to think we've got it all figured out. And, inconveniently, the spirit world doesn't let us do that. The spirit world—even for those of us who know that world is as real as our elbows—is shrouded in mystery. No one is precisely sure how it works. No one. Not the religious master, not the seasoned meditator, not the near-death survivor who's come back to describe the afterlife, not the most brilliant scientist or the most revered guru. No one knows *exactly* how the realms beyond this one operate; no one has the rule book. This makes lots of cuspers so uncomfortable they choose to just deny the whole metaphysical package. It feels safer that way.

But hiding out in the constraints of that artificial safety comes at such personal cost, diminishing the richness of your life experience to a fraction of what it could be.

If you've felt the restriction of disbelief, I invite you now to set aside your desire for hard-line facts just long enough to taste the mystery of surrendering to a force so powerfully satisfying, juicy, and in-your-bones *right* that it's worth giving up your plebeian need for black-and-white answers. Because once you taste this Technicolor force, you never go back. Once you taste it, you understand that its inherent mystery is not a flaw, but just another facet of its irreproachable perfection.

The only important question before you right now is this: Would you *like* to live in a world of miracles, governed by a love this powerfully embracive and all encompassing? If so, it's available to you. Your beliefs are a choice. As Einstein has pointed out, your experience of the world you live in is also a choice.

Most of the contributors to this compilation are no different from you. They aren't any more innately psychic, or energetically sensitive, or wise, or spiritually talented than you are. There's just one thing they have in common: they believe that miracles like the ones found in these pages are possible. You'll hear some of them say they didn't believe until it happened to them, but I would argue that on some subterranean level a thread of belief ran through each of them—a vein of hopefulness that the universe, in all its mind-blowing complexity, is not only friendly, but rooted in a love so far beyond our comprehension that it defies the constructs of our limited present-day paradigms.

You have that same thread running through you or you wouldn't have picked up this book. If you'd like to experience the kinds of things these courageous, vulnerable contributors have experienced, nurture the thread. Make room in your heart for miracles. Pull on the thread until it unravels those hardened, crusty layers of cynicism that only serve to cut you off from the wellspring of infinite, pure love you're made of.

Dip into the well and see how right and natural it feels to join the ranks of the believers. Welcome home. We've been waiting for you.

⚬ 1 ⚬

Spirit Strings

James Van Praagh

It began as most Thursdays do: an ordinary, slight breeze floated over the ocean as the sun moved to find its place in the sky. But I have come to learn that there are rarely any "ordinary" days for someone like me, one who is able to communicate with souls no longer inhabiting this physical dimension. This particular day would send my mystical head spinning into unseen connections, spirit manipulations, and two worlds colliding. This day, the realization that the spirit world is pulling strings to let us know that it is still a very intricate part of our everyday lives struck me like an anvil.

It all started with a forwarded e-mail. A woman named Elaine White had given a speech to a sold-out crowd in Austin, Texas, and she'd mentioned my name. Joyce Elaine White was raised as a Southern Baptist and longed to be a missionary so she could share her faith around the world. She married a man with similar ambitions, and in the nineties Elaine became the executive director of the Capital City Christian Coalition in Austin and a lobbyist for the Christian Coalition in the state capitol. She even cohosted a two-hour show on Christian radio. Two of the main issues of the Christian Coalition were opposing abortion and gay rights.

I didn't know the name Elaine White when I received the e-mail that Thursday, but I soon learned that our experiences could not have been more dissimilar. Just as Elaine was having great success with her work with the Texas far right, I was volunteering at Norman Lear's left-leaning nonprofit, People For the American Way (PFAW). At the same time, I was making my living doing private readings as a professional medium and working on my first book, *Talking to Heaven*. I had also just begun dating my boyfriend (and now husband), Brian. It would be many years later that the earth fell out from under Elaine and steered us toward our meeting.

In early 2011, Elaine's son, Josh, was due to travel to the Middle East for work. Josh was a globe-trotting, Indiana Jones type, and this trip was not so different from others he had been on. Elaine and Josh had dinner at a restaurant before he left, and as they embraced in the parking lot, Elaine heard a voice inside her head that said, *This is your last hug*. Elaine dismissed the voice as the protest of a loving mother whose son was traveling to a region of the world that had been occupying headlines for weeks with news of the Arab Spring.

Ten days later, Elaine was about to start preparing dinner. She was wearing her apron that said "The Queen of Everything," which was the nickname Josh had bestowed upon her. The phone rang. It was the unmistakable voice of her former mother-in-law.

"Have you talked to anybody?"

"What are you talking about?" asked Elaine.

"Oh . . ." Josh's grandmother said. "There was a plane crash. Nobody made it."

Elaine went numb as the horrible story unfolded: The plane that Josh was in had crashed during takeoff from the United Arab Emirates en route to Saudi Arabia. Josh was dead on the other side of the world.

An agonizing eight days later, Josh's body was returned to Dallas in a pine box with his name written on top with black marker. Elaine drove up from her home near Houston and went to the airport with her cousin Randy, who owned a mortuary in town. As they were driving from the airport to the funeral home, Elaine said, "Randy, I'm a strong woman. I know there was a fire after the crash, but I need to see my boy's body. Anything. A finger. A toe."

The next morning, Randy told Elaine that he was not going to allow her to put herself through a viewing. But he did have a keepsake for her: Josh had grown a beard to blend in better in the Middle East, and Randy had saved some of Josh's whiskers for her. Elaine now keeps a few strands of her son's hair in a beautiful silver pendant.

The service was a particularly sad affair, and Elaine had special bookmarks made with Josh's photo and a Bible verse that she passed out to those in attendance. During the burial, as Josh's coffin was being lowered into the ground, Elaine knew that she could no longer be the Queen of Everything. If she were, she would've stopped Josh from leaving in the first place.

After the funeral, the family went out for lunch to Olive Garden. The waiter appeared and said, "Hello, my name is Josh. I'll be your server today." Elaine lost it. That evening, they went to Morton's for dinner. The waiter appeared and said, "Hi, my name is Josh. I'll be your server tonight." What was happening?

Several days after she returned home Elaine's computer was acting up, so she called the Geek Squad to come out. They assured her that a technician would be dispatched, and when she opened the door for the young man a while later, he said, "Hi, my name is Joshua. I'm here to help you with your computer."

The following year was very tough for Elaine. Christmas was tough. Birthdays were tough. About a year after Josh's death, Elaine decided to go to a conference put on by the Omega Institute in New York.

In her first workshop, "Women & Happiness: The Give & Take of Finding Joy," Elaine found herself in a room of about a thousand women. Despite having amonth them several well-known and respected women writers and speakers, Elaine realized it was not making her happy. She went to the organizer of the event and asked if she might try a different workshop instead.

"Sure, that's fine," said the organizer. "I can get you into the James Van Praagh workshop 'Touching the Unseen World: Discovering Your Spiritual Self.'"

Elaine didn't recognize the name.

"He's a famous psychic," the organizer said.

At an earlier time in her life, Elaine had thought that psychics and mediums were somehow demonic. That was what she had been taught during her fundamentalist upbringing. But Elaine's belief system had been evolving for some time. A close family member had had an abortion and Elaine took care of her. Her cousin came out as gay and then became an Episcopal priest. As Elaine was deciding whether to attend the event, a thought crossed her mind: *Well, even Jesus talked to Moses and Elijah on the Mount of Transfiguration. How could it be bad?* She decided to go for it and found a seat among the three hundred participants.

I've done many readings from the stage, and I didn't remember this particular one very well. So I had to ask Elaine what transpired. She said that I introduced myself to the crowd and told them a little about myself and how I worked. I said that everything is energy and that energy never dies; it just changes form. When the physical body dies, the energy that was our consciousness survives, and I had the ability to access it. But I didn't choose whom I communicated with—I was chosen. People aren't so different after they leave the physical world. If you were outgoing and a good communicator here on earth, chances are you'll still be a good communicator afterward.

After I had done a few readings for women in the audience, Elaine heard me say, "I want to talk to the mother of Joshua. He traveled the world, spoke several languages, and was a bit of a wiseacre." Elaine stood up on trembling legs.

I told Elaine that Josh didn't want her to be upset— that it was his time, and he was now with his sister. *What sister?* Elaine thought. Then she remembered the miscarriage she had had when Josh was a little boy. Even back then, Josh had thought it was a little girl. But what really got Elaine's attention was when I said, "Josh is putting a tiara on your head. And you know what that means!" She burst out crying . . . The Queen of Everything!

After the event, Elaine's mind was in a whirl. *Had this really just happened? How could James know these things if he wasn't communicating with Josh?* By this time she was famished and took herself out for dinner. She smiled when her server, Josh, introduced himself. She had a very peaceful meal knowing that her son, the wiseacre, had finally gotten through to her. Josh was pulling strings from heaven and Elaine finally felt the tug.

Elaine now looks forward to getting Josh's signs. On the third anniversary of Josh's death, February 27, Elaine and her husband made the drive from Houston to Dallas to visit Josh's grave. They spent all afternoon on a blanket beside it and then headed back the next day. It was then that Elaine noticed their car's registration tags had expired three months prior. *Please don't let us get a ticket on the way home*, she silently prayed, vowing to take care of the oversight first thing in the morning.

True to her word, Elaine went to the DMV the next day. But when she finally got her turn at the counter, the clerk was not pleased. "Have you been driving this car since December?" the clerk asked with attitude. After Elaine explained her recent loss and the reason for the oversight, the clerk changed her tone and proceeded to process the registration. As Elaine was waiting, her eyes wandered around the clerk's cubicle and locked onto her son's face. Pinned to the wall was one of the bookmarks Elaine had made in Josh's honor for his funeral.

"Where did you get that bookmark?" Elaine asked.

The puzzled clerk turned around and said, "A coworker gave it to me. I was going through a really hard time in my life, and it has given me a lot of courage. The verse on it always puts me in a good mood."

Elaine explained that the person on the bookmark was her son. Awed and humbled, the clerk made the rest of the transaction as pleasant as possible. Josh was pulling strings again.

Elaine likes to be away from home on Josh's birthday, April 23, and on holidays. She knew she had quite a story to tell—of her journey from Christian fundamentalism to a more open, accepting faith; and of her son's constant reminders that he really hasn't gone away—and she contemplated the possibility of sharing her story through public speaking.

Elaine wanted to tell her story with humor, so she decided to contact Judy Carter, author of *The Comedy Bible* and *The Message of You*. Elaine had used Judy's comedy principles back when she was in sales. Elaine hired Judy to coach her, and before she knew it, she was in one of Judy's workshops in Los Angeles. Judy is a hilarious comic who happens to be gay and Jewish, and the two became fast friends. Before long, Elaine found herself telling her story onstage in Austin.

Which brings us back to that seemingly ordinary day that a video of Elaine's speech arrived in my inbox. Elaine and I have since spoken about her journey of faith and transformation. She was open and helpful with all the parts of her story that I hadn't known. We plan on having dinner soon during my next trip to Texas.

In my teachings, I often mention a quote from Albert Einstein: "Coincidence is God's way of remaining anonymous." Elaine's story is too incredible to be fiction. Isn't it possible that the spirit world and our loved ones who reside there can in some way affect our lives in this physical dimension? And doesn't it make sense that the strong connection that Elaine and Josh had in the physical would continue even though Josh is no longer physically here?

Energy doesn't die. Especially the energy of love, which is what we are all made of. Our loved ones don't stop loving us when they pass out of the physical world into the spirit world. In fact, because their energy is no longer focused through the three dimensions of their human brains, they are able to be closer to us than when they inhabited a body. They are Omnipresent. They Nurture us. Their Energy never dies. We are ONE.

❧ 2 ❧

Only Kindness Matters

Sunny Dawn Johnston

Just a few hours into a hospice volunteer training, we were given our first assignment: Write your own obituary. All of us, except for one big, bearded biker guy, went out to write among the red rocks of Sedona. This man, Tim, looked scary, actually, but as I wondered what had brought him into hospice work, I heard Spirit answer with the term "gentle giant." When Tim rejoined us after stealing a smoke break behind one of the buildings, I offered him some paper for his obituary. With the nicotine still on his breath, he said to me, "I'm not writing no fuckin' obituary. I don't even want one when I die." And with that, our friendship began.

Over the next twelve years, I would come to appreciate our soul connection. Tim and I would ebb and flow into each other's lives. He would come to some of my classes, see me for private sessions, and show up at events here and there. Each time I would see him, my heart would expand a little more. Tim lived hard and played hard—and I *loved* his spirit and his spunk and his tell-it-like-it-is nature. He was an inspiration, a challenge, a teacher, and a student—all at the same time. Most of all, Tim was dedicated to being of service.

Over the years, I got to know Tim's family and some of his friends as well. He would teach classes at my healing center once in a while. It was a joy to see him in the role that fit him so well, and that truly did fill him up.

Years passed, and one day he came in to see me for a private session. When I walked in, I could feel that something was wrong; and as I sat down with him, my spirit knew. Tim shared with me that he had been placed on hospice care. The years of playing hard had finally caught up with him, and his heart was only functioning at 15 percent. We sat and talked. Tim loved his family and was afraid to leave them, as he did not want to think of the grief they would have to live through to go on without him. I'd never seen Tim cry before, but that day he did, and as he cried, I could tell he was in his head rather than in his heart. So, I put my hand on his heart and called his attention there. "Okay, my friend, it is okay to feel sadness. But let's listen to what your heart, your spirit, has to say. What do you choose to focus on? Your fear, or your love?"

He responded with a question for me. "What is going to happen, Sunny? Am I going to die?"

I responded, "Yes, Tim, you are going to die; but not on my shift . . . not anytime soon."

A week later we found ourselves back in Sedona— I was presenting at a hospice fund-raiser, and Tim and his wife were special guest attendees. The rough and tough biker I had met eleven years ago now resembled more of that gentle giant, as my spirit had referred to him. No longer able to walk on his own, Tim's loyal wife Teri stayed by his side, pushing his wheelchair. His body was weakening, but his spirit was still strong. During the event, I invited Tim up onstage to share what it was like for a hospice volunteer to be on the other side of the bed. His sharing led to applause and tears.

A year passed without much communication, which again wasn't uncommon for Tim and me. Our spirits were always connected, though, so even though we didn't see each other face-to-face we were always "in touch." However, on the same morning that I received a call that one of my longtime students had passed away the day before, I received another message from Spirit. It was very clear: *Go see Tim*. As divine timing would have it, just a few hours after rearranging my schedule, I received an e-mail from Tim's daughter asking if I would come and see him. I told her I would be there on Friday.

It was a beautiful January afternoon when Robin, a dear friend of mine and Tim's, and I headed out to his house. Just before leaving, Spirit guided me to put some archangel coins in my pocket. Four coins were safely tucked away to share with Tim and his family, to remind them that the angels are with them all during these last few days.

We were greeted with many hugs from Tim's wife and daughter and hellos from a bunch of other family members. I was surprised that there were so many people all hanging out in the living room where Tim had set up shop over the last few months of his life. It was as if he was holding court, with everyone gathered around his recliner, taking in every precious moment. As I got through the hellos, I finally saw Tim sitting in his recliner, oxygen mask strapped on, a very different man than the one I had met twelve years earlier. This man was softer, quieter, and afraid.

"Good morning," he said, as I walked over and gave him a hug. He squeezed me—hard. Our souls were happy to see each other again. We chatted about life, family, the weather. After a half hour or so, though, it was time to get down to the nitty-gritty. Tim said, "Sunny, what am I going to do? Am I going to die now?"

I responded with a smile as I got up and took his hand. "Tim, you tell me. What are you going to do? It is up to you, my friend."

He half smiled and half cried. He just wanted an answer, one that I couldn't give him—not yet, anyway. I could feel that his body was tired, that his life force had diminished, and that he was very close to transitioning. Death is such a personal journey, one our physical self struggles to discern. As Tim and I talked about what he was going to do, I watched him move between this world and the next. He would say something very profound and direct, and then he would drift away and mumble. I've been with many people during their transition process, and I have found this dance between two worlds to be perfectly normal, and fascinating to witness.

When he came back, he said, "Sunny, you have black fuzzy circles around your head. They are floating all around you. They are really dark." I knew intuitively that what he was seeing was his own fears manifested, but I waited a bit to share that. I just listened. Eventually, he asked me if I could see them too.

"No," I said. "I can't see them, Tim, but I felt them when I walked in." He looked at me, a bit surprised, as I continued. "They aren't connected to me, my friend. Those are your fears."

"I'm not afraid to die," he said with that tough biker energy of yesteryear. "I've been waiting to graduate for a long time now." Graduation was what Tim called death.

"I hear you, Tim; and yes, you have been waiting for a long time—but it has never been this close before. Are you willing to walk through these fears with me, so that you can make a clear choice as to what you would like to do?"

During the next hour, Tim and I addressed each one of his fears, and as we did, the black fuzzy things around my head drifted away, one by one. One of his biggest fears was about leaving his wife and family. When I asked him if he thought they would be okay, he was silent. I asked them to join us then, and to reassure him, one more time, that they would be all right without him. Although they had told Tim this time and time before, he needed to hear it again—*now*. In this exact moment. They shared how much they loved him, and how he would always be with them. There wasn't a dry eye in the house. It was heart opening to be a witness to this kind of love. But as we talked, there was still something else. Some other fear we hadn't addressed yet. I tuned in and asked Spirit, but I wasn't sure I was receiving the right answer. It didn't seem to make sense.

It turned out that Tim's greatest fear, unbeknownst to any of us, was that he had not served his purpose in life. A man who gave the shirt off his back over and over; sat with people in the transition process for thousands of hours in his life; shared his beliefs and philosophies with anyone who was interested; loved his family and friends unconditionally; taught people about life and love through energy and healing—this amazing man didn't feel as though he had served his purpose. I was shocked and saddened to hear this, and I knew immediately that I had a job to do when I got home. Seeing my gentle giant of a friend with tears in his eyes, and feeling like he had not done enough for mankind, lit a fire within me.

Tim requested pizza for lunch that day, and I intuitively knew it was going to be his last meal with his family. It was time for me to go and let them be present with each other. As we said good-bye, I gave him one of the guardian angel coins I had brought with me, and I told him to remember that although he had given his angels one hell of a good time, he would now be hanging with them, so he was to be on his best behavior. We both giggled. I hugged him one last time, and those giggles turned into tears creeping out the corners of my eyes.

As Robin and I left, I told Teri that Tim would go very quickly—but we both had jobs to do. Her job was to get him into the care center, as I sensed that he would not leave his body until he was out of their house. That part of the plan was already in motion. They were just waiting on doctors and insurance to get him moved. The hope was to be on their way later that evening. That awareness led to the familiar feeling of knowing that the next time I saw everyone they will have lost the person they loved the most. It is a feeling I have never gotten used to.

Robin and I walked down the sidewalk to our car arm in arm, crying. I put my warm hand in my pocket and felt the coldness of the other three guardian angel coins. I stopped. "Dang! I forgot to give them their angel coins," I said out loud. That is when I heard Spirit say: *You can give them out at the funeral.* Chills ran through me, and I put my trust in Spirit. As Robin and I drove home, we talked about the presence of Spirit alongside us throughout all of the afternoon's events. It was so amazing to witness Tim shifting from one side of the veil to the other. But most of all, we both could not get over the fact that in all of his life's work, he still didn't feel like he had done enough. There was urgency in the air when I arrived home. I was hungry, but I didn't eat. I needed to put my plan into place right away. I sat down in my office, pulled out my iPhone, and with dried tears and a heart full of love I created a video and posted it to my blog, where I knew many of Tim's students, clients, friends, and family would see it. In the video, I asked them to share any thoughts, feelings, or experiences that they had with Tim, to show how he had touched the lives of those around him. I asked Teri to share these messages with Tim while he was still in physical form so that he could see the impact he'd had on the world and know that he had fulfilled his purpose. It only took a few minutes before the first messages began coming in . . .

. . . and in . . .

. . . and in . . .

It was approximately 11:00 p.m. when Teri and Tim were settled into his new space at the care center. She climbed into bed with him and played the video so they could watch it together. Then she read the messages, each and every one of the many loving comments about Tim and his service to humanity. Stories of his love, support, kindness, service, and how he had made an impact on their lives. People who didn't even know Tim commented on how inspiring it was that he had been such a healer in the world through his hospice work. A few minutes later, Tim took his last breath, graduating with honors from this physical world.

While driving to Tim's celebration of life, I remembered that I wanted to share those other guardian angel coins with the rest of Tim's family. But I couldn't find the coins anywhere. I looked and I looked. I dumped my entire purse out to search for them, but they were nowhere to be found. I was heartsick. It was really important to me to give them each an angel coin, just as I had given one to Tim a couple weeks earlier. I frantically searched my purse one more time. Nothing. *Give it up*, I heard as I got out of the truck, feeling defeated. A chill was in the air, so I put on my brand-new coat and began the walk up the driveway. As we approached the house, I put my hands in my coat pockets.

To my joyful surprise, there were four angel coins in the pocket of a coat I had not even worn yet.

"Thanks, Tim," I said out loud with a smile on my face.

I had been asked to officiate the service, and I began with a "Good morning!" Tim had used this greeting for everyone, at any time of day. In fact, the first time I met him at our Sedona retreat, he had introduced himself with a bright "Good morning," which I hadn't found odd since it had been morning. But there was another reason Tim always used this greeting in particular. For Tim, it was always a good morning, because regardless of the time of day, you could always choose to turn your day around. You could start your day over at any time. With Tim's help and guidance, we created a beautiful service full of stories about him and his life. When we came to the part in the service where I would usually read the obituary, knowing Tim, I instead chose to share the story of our first meeting.

"I don't want no fuckin' obituary when I die. I don't want people making things up about me after I am gone. I want to hear them while I am alive," he'd said so many years ago.

Tim then followed with this message to us all: "Tell the people that you love just how much you love them, why you love them, and share from an open heart, in that moment. Don't ever miss a chance to say 'I love you.' And in the end, only kindness matters."

As I walked over to the patio of the pig roast celebration (apropos for the gentle giant Tim, a self-proclaimed roast master), there sat a beautiful wooden bench for everyone to sign. Painted on the bench were those same words I had just said a few moments earlier, as guided by Tim: In the end, only kindness matters.

⮜ 3 ⮞

All That Matters

Lisa McCourt

One of the best conversations I ever had with my mom took place the week after she died. We talked about all the inherent stickiness of the mother-daughter dynamic and the many ways that stickiness had shown up for us. We talked about how a lifetime of misunderstanding one another on many levels had nonetheless never diluted the fierce love that had always underscored our dance together.

Being a long-avowed metaphysics junkie, I had never doubted that I'd have such dialogues with my mom, cross-dimensionally, after her passing. But no matter how many spiritual books I shared with her ninety-year-old grieving mother—my grandmother, Polly—or how many workshops I brought Polly to, nothing made a dent in her crippling anguish over having outlived her precious only daughter.

Polly had named her baby girl Bettye with the special spelling because, in Polly's words, "she was so very special." The two of them had lived together, inseparable, for over a decade before Bettye died. With all the energy of my grief being channeled into consoling Polly, I made personal peace relatively quickly with my mom's transition. Everything had instantly become about my grandmother and finding ways to help her through the most intense emotional suffering I'd ever witnessed in a person.

During my "conversations" with my spirit mom, I would beg her to connect with her mother the way she did with me. I was desperate for Polly to understand that love is bigger than paltry life/death delineations; that love crosses dimensions, and love is all that matters. From her spirit world, my ever-saucy mom would shrug her shoulders and explain that our continuing relationship was only possible because I was so open to it. She seemed to be saying, "It's here if Polly wants it, but that's not up to me."

On this plane, Bettye had been an exceptionally glamorous woman. Shortly before her death, she had given me her stunning pave diamond earrings as a birthday gift. They were earrings she wore every day, her grocery-shopping earrings. Sternly, she'd told me, "These are not to be saved for special occasions. Wear them all the time, like I've done. You're worth that."

Her admonishment had not been unfounded. Though she'd begun giving me a special piece of her jewelry for my birthday each year, I seldom wore these heirlooms. I cherished them; they simply didn't fit into my flip-flop, sundress lifestyle, and I never wanted to chance losing them. Bettye had disapproved wholeheartedly, and she let me know it often while still in her earth body.

Not long after her passing, I pulled out the "everyday" diamond earrings for a formal event I'd been invited to. I tested the safety catch to make sure there was no possible way they could leap off my ears, then enjoyed a carefree evening of dining and dancing. When I got home, only one earring remained. I frantically searched the car, the house, and then the event venue. I made countless phone calls. It was simply gone, even though in every photo of me both earrings were there. Brokenhearted, I called on Spirit-Mom to confess my fiasco.

She rolled her eyes. "I told you not to save them, dumbass," she chuckled, wagging a well-manicured finger at me. "You missed a hundred chances to wear them! Here's what I want you to do now: Take the one earring you still have to my jeweler, Paul. Have him put it on that gold choker chain I gave you, and then *wear* the damn thing, okay?"

I did as she requested and have worn the necklace ever since. Considering that this all took place the week before my birthday, it wasn't hard to figure out what she was up to. With that oh-so-familiar mischievous gleam in her eye, she confirmed my suspicion. "I had to find *some* way to give you a birthday present," she quipped, her satisfied laughter echoing through my energy field.

Polly was unimpressed. "You just lost it," she said, coming to the conclusion shared by most earthbound, logic-inclined people. But I—sporting my gorgeous new birthday gift—knew exactly who had stolen it right out of my ear and why.

Every few months, something similar to the lost-earring scenario would occur. I work and play in spiritual and metaphysical circles, so my friends and colleagues lovingly applauded all accounts of my Spirit-Mom connections. But when I shared these same stories with Polly, I'd suddenly go inexplicably awkward. Why was the one person I most longed to comfort with this information the one I had the most trouble sharing it with? I'd get tongue-tied, emotionally conflicted. Was I in denial, never having properly processed my mom's death? Was I just looking for attention? As real as it felt, was I making it all up? Was it insensitive of me to approach a woman so deeply in mourning with my whimsical game? Was it sacrilege? Was I not properly honoring my mom's passing?

I believe that Polly *wanted* to believe. But she was a daily-Bible-reading, former Sunday school teacher who simply would not entertain concepts she perceived to fall outside the boundaries of her beloved faith. I could tell she painfully envied my continued connection with Bettye while simultaneously refusing to accept it.

Despite this hurdle, my relationship with Polly continued to deepen, and her crushing sadness gradually began to lift. We had fun together. We went on weekly adventures, from acupuncture appointments to vegetable shopping. When she was invited to her great-niece's wedding, she asked me to take her.

It was a long drive, up the entire state of Florida, but we had mapped out our stops and provisioned with car snacks, music, and an audiobook I wanted her to hear called *The Afterlife of Billy Fingers* by Annie Kagan.

Early in the book, a coin was presented as a special sign from "the other side." Stopping at our first rest area, I opened the car door to find a shiny penny smiling up at me. I picked it up and showed Polly.

"See? Mom gave us a coin. She's listening to the book with us, and this is her way of telling you to pay attention!" Though my tone was light, in my heart I knew my words to be true.

Spirit-Bettye continued to play with us for the rest of the nine-hour drive. A meaningful string of songs on the radio . . . an employee name tag at the next rest stop . . . an order of her favorite dish "accidentally" brought to our table during dinner. I gently, teasingly pointed out each "coincidence" to Polly, who'd just shake her head at me with wistful eyes and a tolerant smile.

I went into private communion with Bettye and said, "C'mon, Mom, is this the best you can do? It's clear to me you're on this trip with us, but could you manage something a little more convincing for her?"

My fiery, beautiful mom was never one to back down from a challenge.

We at last arrived at the home of Polly's baby brother, and after much resting and visiting it was time to get ready for the wedding. I helped Polly into her fancy dress and then perched on the edge of the bathroom tub to marvel at her still-skillful makeup application.

Her soft smile vanished as she began rooting through her makeup bag with a furrowed brow. "Oh, no. Oh, no. I didn't bring it," she moaned.

"Bring what?"

"My lipstick. Oh, I hate to go to the wedding without any lipstick. Do you think there's enough time for you to run out and get me some?"

"It'll be tight," I said, rushing to get my car keys. As I grabbed them, sunlight from the window reflected off something shiny and unfamiliar in my open suitcase. Going in for a closer look, I realized it was a silver lipstick case. I don't wear lipstick and had never bought or owned such a thing. I grabbed it and took it to Polly.

"I know it's a long shot, but I found this lipstick in my suitcase. I have no idea where it came from, and it's probably all wrong, but I'm showing it to you just in case it could work."

Polly examined the tube. "That's my brand. That's my color. Where did you get this?"

"I told you; it was in my suitcase. I didn't see it when I packed at home or when I unpacked here, so you must have brought it after all and somehow it ended up in my luggage instead of yours."

She opened the tube. It was barely used. "No," she whispered. "The lipstick I've been using was almost all worn down to nothing. This is practically new. I haven't bought a new tube in years."

The goose bumps erupting across my body left no doubt in my mind as to what was going on. Always-fashionable Bettye had been a passionate makeup enthusiast—much more so than either her daughter or mother. To her, lipstick had been as necessary as oxygen.

I dared not speak a word of my realization out loud, afraid that it would be too much for Polly. Afraid I was pushing her too far. Afraid she would think I'd set this up somehow.

But I didn't have to speak it. She looked up at me and softly said, "It was Bettye, wasn't it?"

I took her hand. "I believe it was."

Her tiny frame trembled, then steadied with a slow, deep breath.

Through tears, she said, "It was . . . It is . . . I can feel her here."

My mom has never since communicated with quite that degree of dramatic flair. But she hasn't needed to.

Because Polly knows now, as utterly as I do.

Today, the new lipstick sits on Polly's dresser right next to the old tube she'd forgotten to pack. We hear songs sent specifically to us. We find messages in coins and clouds and flowers. We dream her face, we smell her perfume in improbable places, we hear her infectious, devil-may-care laugh in the laugh tracks of corny TV shows.

And we know. Together now, we know.

☞ 4 ☜

The Real Deal

Chelsea Hanson

As I approached the thick, single-glass door of the brick office building on the way to my appointment, I felt hopeful, but also unsure. I'd even considered canceling, thinking I should have stayed home rather than drive through the snow on such a dreary day.

Once inside, I was calmed a bit by the gentle sound of the trickling water fountain in the entryway. The angel figurines and framed diplomas on the walls comforted me in an odd way amid the office tableau of haphazardly placed furniture, overgrown plants, and two messy piles of magazines.

Right away, Trish welcomed me into her office with a nervous, curious laugh. She invited me to sit in one of the two overstuffed chairs, and I sank into the olive green one, its nubby material scratchy beneath me.

Even though I didn't know what to expect, I'd booked Trish for an angel therapy session. I'd found her through an article regarding hypnotherapy in a natural health magazine. Earlier in the year, I'd experienced a hypnobirthing session with Trish when I was pregnant with my son, Jacob.

We chatted briefly to catch up. And then without further preamble about how our session would proceed today, Trish asked, "Who died from heart problems?"

Wow! Such a direct, pointed question to begin, I thought.

"My father died in open-heart surgery when I was four years old," I replied.

Trish seemed perplexed. "The man I see looks older and has gray hair, wears glasses, and is reading the newspaper."

"Well . . . that could be my dad. He looked older than he was when he died," I said.

In truth, I didn't know whether my father wore glasses or read the newspaper because I knew little about him. He died in open-heart surgery in 1972 when he was only forty-one. His death left my mom a widow, a single parent with a four-year-old and a business to run. Mom rarely talked about Dad because it was too painful. She didn't want to upset me when I was growing up because her goal was to protect me, her only child. I faintly remember my father's voice and what he looked like. But not much else. My father's life was a mystery to me because my mother never spoke of him.

Trish seemed satisfied with my answer and was oddly confident she was talking about my father.

"Do you ever feel someone touching your hand?" she asked.

"Yes, I do remember that sensation. It's been a while, though," I said. The last time I had had this experience was when I was a freshman in high school. I felt a light tingling on my forearm with little pinpricks that didn't hurt. I hadn't thought about what it was or meant since. But now here I was, thirty-four years after his death, receiving affirmation that my dad might have connected with me. Was it possible my father's spirit was coming through Trish?

I didn't think about my father much, but I thought about my deceased mom a lot.

"Who couldn't breathe or talk?" Trish asked. "I feel like I'm suffocating, as if something is in my throat."

I felt tightness in my throat too.

"My mother couldn't communicate with me when she was dying because she was too weak," I said. Was it possible Trish was experiencing how my mother felt when she died?

Mom had died ten years earlier, when I was twenty-eight. Although the grief had lessened over the years, the loss was always with me. The sadness had intensified again a few months ago after the birth of my son. It just didn't seem possible, nor fair, that Mom wasn't present during such an important milestone in my life. Believing that she'd never get to see or meet my firstborn was like living her death all over again.

Tears streamed down my face as Trish allowed me to take in what she'd said. I felt the ripple of a chill up my spine.

How did Trish know these things? There was no way she could know how my mother died and the details of her death. Was it possible Trish could communicate with my parents? I was stunned by the information she was giving me, and yet gladdened that it was possible I was in communication with my mother. Right here, right now, with Trish as my channel. Because I wanted to connect with my mom so much, I pushed away my incredulity. I wanted to believe Trish was connecting to the spiritual realm and bringing my parents back to me.

Trish was ready to move on. "There's a rabbit. I'm seeing a rabbit." And she described it.

At first, I had no idea what this sign meant.

"I'm not sure . . . I've always liked rabbits. In fact, I've decorated my home with vintage-looking rabbits and figurines . . ." My voice trailed off. The message didn't seem correct.

"Tell me more," Trish encouraged.

"Oh!" I got excited. "You must mean the plush animal with brown floppy ears, movable arms and legs, long whiskers, and loopy yarn fur. The one I bought last month when my best friend and I spent 'girl time' together."

Could it be this rabbit was coming through as a sign to validate Mom witnessed this happy moment with my friend and was pleased? Yes, my inner knowing said. This was absolutely the correct interpretation of the bunny sign!

For over an hour, Trish connected with my deceased loved ones and shared her visions. This was the *real deal*. As she asked me questions and I filled in details, my emotions ran the gamut from surprised to shocked to dumbfounded at all that was coming through.

I had no idea Trish was capable of obtaining messages from the spiritual realm. My expectation for our session today had been a traditional therapy session. Perhaps talk therapy to help me handle my grief better since it had resurfaced after my son's birth. I hadn't known it was possible to make such a connection and communicate with someone who had died.

Suddenly, it all added up. I'd experienced these "visits" from my parents—Mom especially—off and on throughout my life. Being a busy professional in a corporate role, I'd brushed them off as woo-woo. I decided in that moment I had nothing to lose. I'd set aside my disbelief and pay attention when I got these hits, signs, or hunches from now on.

I'd missed both my parents. But now I felt so much lighter, knowing I had an eternal, continuing bond with my loved ones.

Months passed, and it was the Christmas season. Because Mom had died right before Christmas, I'd never celebrated this time of year with joy. I'd even made a habit of not looking forward to it during the past ten years. But this year was different. I had a new baby. And since Christmas is about the celebration of birth and new life, perhaps it was possible this season could be different. I was open to a sign.

One evening, while sitting in Jacob's room, I looked around and realized how lucky I was to have this child. After two miscarriages I wasn't sure I would ever have a family of my own, and now I did.

This baby's room was warm and comforting, the walls a faux finish with a lovely combination of blue, yellow, and light pink that I painstakingly selected in order to create the perfect room for my child. The blue-sky ceiling played off the white wooden rocker, crib, dresser, and bookshelf filled with fun kids' books. This was a room I would have loved to have shown to Mom.

I got an intuitive hit to listen to Sarah McLachlan, my favorite singer since Mom had passed. Sarah's latest CD, *Winter Song*, had just come out, and I popped it into Jacob's music player and listened as we snuggled on the floor. "Have Yourself a Merry Little Christmas" came on, and upon hearing the chorus, I knew.

This was it. The sign. Mom's spirit telling me to go on. That it was okay to enjoy Christmas again, especially with my new child.

Christmas had arrived early that year—the day I banished self-doubt and entered Trish's office, the day she showed me that indeed it IS possible to continue to connect and communicate with my loved ones. Forever. And that was the best gift of all.

⪻ 5 ⪼

Constance

Kristen Marchus-Hemstad

As a child, I was scared of everything; there wasn't one day that passed without me being terrified of seemingly my own skin. The world around me seemed porous, like anything could come through my walls or windows at a moment's notice.

As I grew, so did my discomfort—not just in the world around me, but also being in my own skin. I didn't look like all the other petite, tanned girls in my school; and I felt that I could feel and know their judgmental thoughts without them even needing to say them aloud. On the rare occasion that I looked into the mirror, my face appeared to change, morph into different adult faces. Seeing another female or male face superimposed over my own was incredibly shocking! Whenever that happened, I would ask, "Who are *you?*" and "What do *you* want?" Eventually my face would come back, but not before I wondered if I was losing my mind.

Additionally, I started beginning to feel my "self" separate or come out of my body whenever I was in a large group, open spaces, or tight quarters. During these episodes, my surroundings felt unreal, and I felt like I was losing my mind, going to die, or would somehow evaporate. I felt trapped, like I *had* to get out of the situation or hide or else I would be killed. Finally, I confided in my parents, and they supported me by helping to find a mental health team. I was diagnosed with panic attacks and depression and was prescribed medications, therapy, and biofeedback. The treatments helped some of the symptoms, but I wanted to know the core issue.

Despite the continuance of my depression through college, I married a wonderful man, graduated with a master's degree in counseling, and landed a great job as a crisis worker at a psychiatric hospital. All seemed the blueprint for a great life.

However, my dark mood persisted and my stress increased, and I became extremely ill. The diagnosis was fibromyalgia, and my body felt broken, with weird pains such as throbbing bruises on my back that no one else could see, my arms feeling like they were being pulled out of their sockets, sinus infections, and panic attacks.

Thankfully my doctor was open-minded, and when I asked him about alternative and spiritual therapies, he said, "Well, there are things that Western medicine can't explain. I know that God has created other therapies, and if I didn't believe that there were other explanations, I could not do my job."

I knew that this pain was coming from Spirit, as a direct line to guide me in a different direction than the path I was headed down. When I didn't listen, it pushed harder—but when I surrendered to Spirit, the pain lessened, and my life improved.

The pain and fatigue from my fibromyalgia became manageable after I switched career paths to work at a software company. The panic attacks and anxiety, however, were another story. These would come and go in waves, particularly when I was in a car, and they reared their ugly heads when I was driving on the interstate, sitting in congested traffic, or waiting in turning lanes. I felt trapped when wearing a coat or seatbelt, which I had to unbuckle just to keep moving. Even riding as a passenger in a car became unbearable. I had to put my head down on the center console with my husband's hand on my head to make even a short car ride. The feeling that if I didn't hide or keep moving I was going to die returned, and with vehemence. Occasionally, I could not even leave my house because of the anxiety and wound up sitting alone in my dark closet.

After trying everything from homeopathic doctors, to spiritual readings, to regression therapy, and everything in between, I finally found a wonderful intuitive counselor.

During one of our sessions, she looked at me very curiously and said, "Kristen, you know you have come here to do medium work, right?"

I automatically said, "Well, of course I have," and suddenly backpedaled when I realized what I had said. "What?! I am not special enough to be a medium!"

Her answer was, "Who says? Why someone else and not you? Who says you are not special enough?"

With this revelation, so many of my experiences started to make sense, and initially I was ecstatic. Many of my family members and friends supported me, but not everyone. There were some harsh blows from those who sat in judgment of my ability. One friend told me I was going to hell and there was a battle for my soul. My family and I even received DVDs in the mail—with no return addresses—containing programs declaring that mediums are evil.

This backlash was too much for me. I had always been emotionally sensitive, and I was ready to stop developing my gift until I found Kevin Schoeppel's book, *The Bible: The Truth About Psychics & Spiritual Gifts*. Since reading the book, Schoeppel and I have developed a friendship, and his support has been life changing. His knowledge of scripture helped me to realize that being a medium is a gift from God.

The more I investigated and became comfortable with my psychic gifts and mediumship, the more my anxiety improved. However, that insistent panic unfortunately remained, and my body's reaction was totally out of proportion for the situation. My heart knew being a medium was a gift, but thoughts of "you are going to hell" continued.

Finally, angry and fed up with my inability to rid myself of the paralyzing panic, I put my hands up and said, "Okay, God, I am doing what I think you are guiding me to do; but stepping into my abilities as a medium isn't the entire answer. I am done struggling! I am done! Please help me!"

When I was through feeling sorry for myself, I phoned an intuitive friend, Sharyl. During our conversation, I realized that when I am in the car, I feel the same way as when my face is covered by water, which was also a terrible fear of mine. Then, the words flew from my mouth before I could stop them: "Could this be a past life?" I asked. Sharyl agreed, saying that this was definitely her sense.

Sharyl recommended that I recreate that feeling and have a journal nearby to observe what transpired. I was nervous, but I agreed this would be the best way to find the root of my enigmatic phobia. I drew a warm bath, lit a candle, and then asked God to please help me gain clarity on the cause of the panic and how to relieve it. Lying back in the bath wasn't productive, so I sat up, clasped my hands behind me, allowed my torso to become cold, and then slowly lowered my face into the water. Suddenly, my senses were intensified.

As I came up out of the water, I was quick to grab for my journal. I wrote,

> I am Constance and they are drowning me. I am in
> the water. They drowned me. They are all laughing.
> I want them to stop. I didn't do anything. I am good.
> I am a nurse, good, I am good. Please don't do this to
> me. God sent me here as a member of the clergy—the
> cloth—and holy, to bring peace. I am doing his work. I
> am worthy. I am not a witch or blasphemy. I am good.

I crawled out of the tub, completely exhausted. Based on my intuition and further journaling, I discovered that my guilt and fear of my mediumship came from my past life as Constance, also a medium, where I was brutally punished for my gifts.

I confided in two friends, and their responses validated my experience. One said that she was led to read a book and the main character was named Constance. The other was stunned that on the same night of my experience she'd told her boyfriend, "I can't get the name Constance out of my head. Constance, Constance." That was the moment I abandoned all doubt.

The awareness of this past life was all I needed to shift my thoughts away from judgment, to reinforce that I am good and the panic does not belong to me as Kristen.

Over the subsequent months, I had increased physical sensitivity, pain, and fatigue flare-ups and would lie in bed and sweat. Slowly and gently the pain lessened, and my confidence in myself and my gift increased. Best of all, as I finally embraced my gifts, the panic diminished significantly. I no longer feel that persistent fear I carried like a stack of bricks my entire life. I am no longer that bound and tortured person, feeling like I am drowning while strapped in a car. My body and mind are healing, and I feel blessed for this gift.

Now, I feel firmly attached to my body, and my life as Kristen Marchus-Hemstad is my own. However painful this process has been, these intense feelings were amazing teaching tools. With my true life's purpose finally clear to me, I can move past fear, panic, and judgment and tap into the vast innate knowledge of what it really is to be a medium and help others.

～ 6 ～

Still There

Wendy Kitts

I was a daddy's girl. We shared a love of baseball, old movies, and Johnny Cash. When I was nine, my father came to the hospital to pick me up after I'd had my tonsils out. He'd been living in another province in Canada for almost a year. My first words every morning were, "Is Daddy coming home today?"

That day he showed up, hair slicked back and looking freshly scrubbed and shiny in a suit and tie, is undeniably still engraved in my memory almost fifty years later.

He scooped me out of my hospital bed and carried me out in his strong arms. I exploded with pride as I beamed over his shoulder at the nurses and the other children in the ward.

Daddy was finally home.

As I got older, it was inevitable that one day I would realize that he was not Superman, but superhuman, with all the flaws that come with being so.

I had my own opinions. Opinions he didn't always share. And growing up in an orphanage from the age of four, my father had demons that didn't allow for any of us to get too close.

He was brilliant, especially for only having a grade four education. And he could fix anything; so there were certain things I always went to him for, like how to hook up my cable, or where to go to get my car repaired.

There was a void in my heart when he passed. And in my life. So many times, especially in the first few years, I'd pick up the phone to ask his advice and then realize he was no longer on the other end of the line.

At least not physically.

I believed my father was still around, but I just couldn't see him; however, he made his presence known in other more magical ways.

I knew from reading James Van Praagh's books that manipulating electricity is one of the easiest and most prevalent ways a loved one communicates to us after physical death; so I took comfort in the flickering lights the first few days after his passing. In fact, the lamp next to my mother's bed caused us so much trouble that a friend insisted on checking the wiring in the basement. But I knew nothing wrong would be found, and I took it as a sign that my father was still here, looking out for us.

Then one night, not long after his passing, I was awakened from a deep sleep by his voice in my ear. *Look out the window*, he said. I was tired, so I argued with the voice, which was kind of funny seeing how I often argued with him in life.

But his voice was insistent. *Get up*.

I dragged myself to the window. Dozens of deer were gorging themselves on the fallen fruit from the old apple tree in my parents' backyard.

It was a bad winter that year, the snow deep, so the deer often ventured out of the woods and into the village at night to feast on whatever they could find. My parents would watch them when my father's emphysema prevented sleep.

But never had so many deer come at once before. I rushed to wake my mother. We laughed at their drunken antics, tipsy from overindulging in too many fermented apples, until they staggered home, scattering at first light like vampires back to their coffins.

Flickering lights and midnight deer-spotting aside, usually when I need the most help, I smell the unmistakable scent of Old Spice, my father's cologne, and know he is watching out for me. Dad is also great at arranging green lights and parking spaces. He's so good at getting the best spots that a friend of mine adopted him as her parking genie. I often talk to him while driving, and if I have car trouble, I ask for guidance. He has never failed to answer.

Recently my car needed some work in order to pass its annual safety check. A lot of work. The car was sixteen years old and getting close to the time when it no longer made sense to put any more money into it. I knew that time was dawning, but I felt it still had a few miles to give yet.

When I was told it would take fifteen hundred dollars to pass inspection, I had to make a decision, and I turned to others for confirmation of what I felt was the right choice—to get it fixed. After all, the car was paid for. And if that amount was averaged over a year, it was still cheaper than a monthly car payment.

Though well meaning, my friends and family members felt the car wasn't worth it. The unanimous consensus was that I should give it up and put the money into a new car instead.

I decided to take the night to think about it.

As I drove home sipping the Coke I'd been nursing long before I went to my mechanic's that afternoon, my heart felt torn. I knew what I wanted to do, what my intuition was urging me to do, but why were so many people suggesting the opposite?

My willingness to listen to my intuition, to be guided by it, had always been strong, especially since my father's death. Was it possible everyone else was wrong about what was best for me? Was I strong enough to keep my own counsel and continue to trust when others were certain my mechanic was taking advantage of me?

Over the next couple of hours I talked to a few more people, still hoping someone would agree with me. I wanted to feel justified in my decision. But I got the same responses all over again.

So I did what I usually do when I need clarity. I asked for a sign.

As I sat on my couch staring out the picture window at the early evening sky, I willed my brain to make a decision. I thought about my father and wished he were there to help me. This was exactly the kind of thing I would normally go to him for. And in that moment, I felt like I'd lost him all over again. Tears streamed down my face.

I wiped them away with the back of my hand and reached for the long, warm bottle of Coke in my lap.

That's when I saw it.

I blinked; then burst into tears again.

Happy tears.

The bottle was part of Coca-Cola's "Share a Coke" campaign, which had people's first names printed on the label.

There, in bold white letters against a Coke-red background, was the name Bob—my father's name.

I knew my answer.

I had been looking for father's help with my car—just as I always had when he was alive, and now I had a clear sign that he was listening. Not only that, but that he backed my intuitive decision to get the car fixed, rather than giving up on it wholesale and buying a new one. Even though he passed over nine years ago, I know that I can always reach out to my father. He is still the same hero that he was when I was young, and while his physical body may be gone, his presence is a constant and loving counselor whenever I need guidance.

❧ 7 ❧

Mermaid's Message

Phoenix Rising Star

I had planned the island getaway in hopes that we'd find the inspiration to renew and revive our tired, worn-out marriage. We had drifted apart; or maybe we'd never really been together. I wanted desperately to find a way to get us to a good place, and believed that a change of venue might shift us into a change of heart.

But midway into this vacation onto which I had pinned so many hopes and dreams, I was forced to acknowledge that location made no difference in the way we related to one another or felt about one another.

I wanted to stroll the moonlit beach at night. Joe wanted to watch ESPN.

I wanted to walk along the water's edge at sunrise, watch the birds, and marvel at the beautiful sun sharing its magnificent light on the ocean. Joe wanted to sleep in.

I wanted to talk about angels. He turned up the volume on the TV.

On the day I woke up feeling the most frustrated and hurt, I left the room early to hike the beach alone. I stopped at an isolated patch of shoreline some distance from the resort, found a stick, and drew a sacred circle in the sand. Unable to contain my sadness any longer, I sat in the middle of the circle and wept.

The waves lapped gently on the shore. Even through my personal pain, I was aware of the incredible beauty around me and the sun beaming down on me from the cloudless sky. My heart breaking, I sobbed, "Tell me what to do, God. I don't know anymore what to do, and I want to know so badly!" My head was in my hands, tears streaming down my face and arms.

I heard a voice say, *It's time to leave the relationship*.

I jumped a foot, whipping my head around to see who had replied. I felt so foolish; I hadn't realized I'd spoken out loud. Shocked out of my tears, I looked up and down the beach. No one was there.

Again, I heard the voice say, *It's time to leave the relationship*. Utterly alone on the beach, I realized I was hearing the voice in my head and my heart. It was God, or it was my soul. To me, the two had always been interchangeable.

"No, God. You don't understand," I said firmly. "That is not an option. I did *not* get married only to get divorced. We've been together for over ten years! There has to be another option." With that, I picked up my towel, wiped my face, and walked slowly back to the room, turning my back on God, my sacred circle, and my pain.

Three hours later, I was snorkeling in a shallow area of incredibly clear water. The sunlight was so bright it hurt my eyes as I watched my hand dragging desultorily along the ocean floor. Even when my fingers disturbed the tiny grains of snow-white sand, the water remained crystal clear, and I marveled at the intricate patterns created by the waves and my own fingertips.

Lost in thought, I was jerked out of my reverie by the sight of a small female hand pushing up out of the sand and grabbing my own. I gasped, sending water into my air tube as I wrenched my hand away from her surprisingly strong grip.

Stunned by this bizarre turn of events, I realized that my wedding ring, which had not left my hand in over ten years, had been yanked off my finger. I watched the glittering gold band spiral through the water and then ever so slowly settle on the pristine white sand in front of me. I reached to retrieve it. But it disappeared, sinking out of sight right before my eyes.

Horrified, I fell to my knees and frantically pawed through the sand. What in the world had just happened? My ring! Where was my ring? It was all too absurd to comprehend. It had been right there. I had seen it clearly, and now it was nowhere. Was this God's way of answering my question? It couldn't be!

I stumbled onto the beach, crying, shaken to my core. Joe rushed up to me, full of concern. "What is it?" he asked. "Are you hurt? What happened?"

I couldn't control my hysterical sobbing. "Nothing. And everything! Everything happened! Oh, I can't believe this," I moaned, my tears dripping onto the sand.

Bewildered, Joe continued his line of questioning. He'd never seen me act this way before. Neither had I, for that matter.

"A . . . a hand grabbed mine! In the water!" I stuttered incoherently. "And pulled my ring off! I think I know where it landed, but it disappeared. I have to go back to look for it!"

"A hand? Someone grabbed you? Where is he? I'll kill him!" said Joe, bunching his fists in reaction to the threat.

"No, you don't understand! It wasn't like that. There wasn't anyone there. This was someone under the sand. Someone grabbed my hand. Some female grabbed me and . . . and . . ." I trailed off, seeing the look on his face.

"Never mind," I said, scrambling up to go back to the water. "I'll go look for it. I've got to find it!"

I snorkeled around and around the spot where my ring had fallen. I sifted through the sand, realizing I was likely just making things worse by covering up whatever might be there but unable to come up with any better plan. I had to do all I could to find it. Sunburnt and exhausted after three hours of searching, I finally gave up. The ring was simply not there. And that hand? What was that hand? And why did my ring disappear?

In time, I began to think of the small female hand as the hand of a mermaid, a magical creature sent to deliver a message I had resisted accepting. When I'd heard the loud and clear voice in my sacred circle on the beach, I had turned my back on God, or my soul, whatever term you want to use. I had ignored the message. So something had to be done to get my attention—something too big for me to ignore.

Of course, I can't be sure it was a mermaid. But that tiny female hand had emerged from beneath the ocean floor. I'd felt it grab my hand. It was no coincidence that the symbol of my marriage, my wedding ring, was the casualty of the encounter. It would be hard for anyone to miss the meaning of such a dramatic experience.

I didn't like the message. But in my heart, I knew it was valid. I knew that I was being given a chance at freedom. Freedom to be me. Freedom to live in the way that was right for me.

Free of the opinions and control of others.

I did leave the relationship. Not immediately, but in my way and in my counseling first, then seeing an attorney and moving out. And yes, it was sad. But it was also empowering. And healing. And I believe it was the best thing I could have possibly done. I gifted myself the opportunity to grow, and evolve, and be who I truly am—all thanks to a mermaid!

❧ 8 ❧

Grandma's Gifts

Marla Steele

My grandma was so special to me. She was an independent, charismatic, and compassionate family doctor ahead of her time. She took me camping, fishing, hiking, and canoeing. Not your typical granny stuff. I went on hospital rounds with her where I often hung out in radiology labs with her colleague Dr. Summers, learning how to read X-rays and vowing to never need an upper gastrointestinal test because I saw that nasty barium chalk solution they had to drink.

If some of her patients couldn't afford to pay, she would say, "Just bring me some food from your garden or let my granddaughter ride your horses." That was the best part of visiting Grandma; she did everything in her power to connect me with horses, even when it meant she had to do a two-hour trail ride because I was the only one signed up and she didn't want to send me off into the woods alone with a total stranger. I still remember her trying to walk the next day, a day she decided to reroute our road trip to include a stop in Paducah, Kentucky, so I could meet Secretariat in person.

Many years later she was still making my horse dreams come true. In fact, I believe this was a soul pact that we had, for in the timing of her illness one autumn, I traveled back to the Midwest to visit her in the hospital I had known so well as a youth. On this trip I also met and fell in love with the Arabian that was to be my first horse. I was at Grandma's bedside telling her all about him with a sparkle in my eye. It seemed to lift her spirits too. A few weeks later she gifted me with the funds to have him shipped to my California home. I had exactly two months to renovate the dilapidated barn and make all necessary preparations before he arrived.

The big day came on December 17. It was raining pretty hard, so I ran out to get some last-minute bedding materials for his stall. As I was returning from the feed store I saw a little holographic image of a bluebird fly right through my windshield and land on the dashboard of my truck. I somehow knew it was a divine message from my grandma. It said, "I am fine. I don't need a funeral. It is your busy time at work. Enjoy your horse." Then it took off. I had never experienced anything like that before. I suspected what it meant. Time stood still, and yet it marched on uncontrollably. My horse was due to arrive within the hour.

The biggest dream of my life thus far had manifested. I heard the magical clip-clop coming up the driveway, a sound that sparked more joy than even the ice cream truck coming up the street when I was a child. I was exuberant, eleven on a scale of one to ten. I did not leave my horse's side for hours. I realized it was getting late and I needed to eat. As soon as I entered the house, the phone rang. It was my mom. "Grandma passed earlier this afternoon," she said. "We just got the call."

Of all the days to pass, Grandma cushioned the blow for me. I knew she'd waited for my horse to arrive. It was like the last of her earthly tasks were complete.

But it was not the last I heard from Grandma. She appeared before me several more times, both in my dreams and waking life. She kept me company when I felt lonely. She helped guide me on my current career path and even pulled some strings to help me win a few contests, including a really nice pair of riding pants and a trip to Hawaii. Most meaningfully, Grandma stood by my side to help me assist with my father's transition a few years later. But his cancer and subsequent death weren't the only medical problems my doctor-granny warned me of.

Ten days before it happened I had the dream. I was in the hospital bed feeling a bit of a chill. I kept trying to pull the blanket over my chest, but for some reason it would not stay up. The doctor gave me a shot in my left arm. I really did not want it. I remember telling him so, but I was injected against my will. I felt the hot liquid infusion run deep inside my arm. It was a weird, nervy sensation. I was losing control. *Why were they not honoring my wishes?* I asked. I was searching for my grandma. I looked to the right and saw a woman I had known in the past even though I couldn't make out her face. *Why isn't she helping me?* I wondered. *Can't she hear me?* I woke up in a bit of a panic. This was one of "those" dreams—the real kind.

On Grandma's birthday, December 2, I had planned to meet a friend; but her toddler had a different agenda. So I decided to go to the local market and pick up lunch instead. To my surprise, one of Grandma's signature dishes was there at the buffet: chicken Jerusalem. Now this was definitely a hello from heaven because never before or since have I seen this meal offered. Of course, I had to have it! I silently acknowledged Grandma with a smile and imagined that we were dining together. Then I headed to the barn to treat my paint horse, Sparky.

Sparky had been on rehab for months due to a severe leg injury. He had just graduated from complete stall rest to going for a few walks a day. For a horse used to running and bucking at will, this was torture. The energy gets so bottled up it doesn't take much to blow. Well, on this day something startled him, and he reared straight up. On his way down he cracked the back of my head. I face-planted into the gravel. For a grand finale, he stepped on my back between my shoulder blades. I remember thinking, *Wow, and now you step on me, adding insult to injury,* but at the same time it was so gentle for a thousand-pound horse. I wondered if Grandma was cushioning the blow once again.

Whoever it was, I was definitely protected. It was a miracle that I didn't pass out. Not only did I have a significant amount of blood pouring out of the front and back of my head, but I was also the only person on the property. The owners were out of town, and it would be a few hours before the dinner feeder discovered me. I had the presence of mind to start running some energy frequencies. I also called on the angels to keep me company while I waited for the ambulance to arrive. As the paramedics were laying me on the stretcher I could see Archangel Michael above me, and Grandma and Dad to the side. In this moment of panic, I decided that this would be a "comeback" story for me, one that I would be able to tell with humor and lightness. I also decided that every hand that touched me would be a healing hand of God. I was amazed how my breath shifted and was much deeper and steadier than normal.

I was asleep in the ER until the chill in the air woke me up. I kept trying to pull my shirt up, not realizing it was ripped and could not stay in place. It took me a few moments to recognize a familiar face. It was my husband's. In walked the familiar woman from my dream that I could not place. She was a coworker of my husband's from years ago, and now she was wheeling me in to have an X-ray taken. I kept asking her for a special bib to protect my thyroid, but she said she could not take my neck brace off. I kept reassuring her that my neck was fine and that I was a medical intuitive and knew my body well, but she would not hear me. So I asked Grandma and Dr. Summers to keep me safe from the radiation.

Miraculously, there were no broken bones, just a little broken pride. It was time for the stitches and staples. They had given me a local anesthetic near the wounds, but now they wanted to give me a much stronger pain shot in my left arm. Again, like in my dream, I begged them not to, but they said there was no way I could sit still for them to do their work without it. They were right. I felt the hot liquid melt inside my arm for the second time and realized I must have been shown all of this in advance for a reason. I surrendered to the moment and went limp.

I definitely had my share of angels in heaven and on earth helping me heal my body. During my recovery I asked, how was this injury useful? I believe this is much more powerful than asking *why*. The answer I heard was, *Well it cracked your third eye wide open. You are a real Harry Potter now, and you'll have the scar to prove it!*

They were so right! After the accident, I knew my psychic energy was growing, and my readings got a turbo boost. You see, it wasn't just my grandma's love from both the physical plane and beyond that she gifted me, or her warnings and intuitive guidance as she showed me what to expect from the future; she also gifted me the ability to powerfully connect with my intuition and guidance, and the revelation that these energy gifts were available to me all along. It was certainly no coincidence that I healed in record time. And now, when I do a reading for someone, I know that Grandma is watching and guiding me, and in turn helping me to guide others to their greatest good as well.

Through the Heart of a Child

Shelly Kay Orr

When Poppy was about sixteen months old, she told us a secret we had been keeping from her. She told us about the existence of her brother and sister.

Poppy was standing at the window looking out into the backyard. She became very excited and started jumping up and down.

"Mommy. Daddy. Angel boy! He's shiny!"

I was shocked.

"What, Poppy? What did you say?"

"There, Mommy, back door now," she said, pointing with joy.

My husband and I stared at each other in astonishment.

"I didn't tell her," he said.

"Me neither," I replied, in shock.

A few months after Poppy saw the angel boy in the backyard, she was sitting at the dining room table.

"*Shhh*," she said loudly.

"I wasn't talking."

"Not you. Don't you hear them, Mommy? My brother and sister are running up and down the hallway. They are being too noisy!"

Poppy does have a brother and a sister, twins named Andrew and Kai. Andrew died in utero hours before his birth, and Kai died shortly after birth. To Poppy they are just as alive as they were in my womb. There is no absence to Poppy, only life.

After Poppy told us about her brother and sister, I set out a photo of my husband and me holding the twins. Poppy saw the picture and asked to hold it.

As she looked at it closely, a smile formed across her face.

"They aren't in their bodies anymore, Mommy."

"No, you are right, Poppy" I said. "They aren't."

"They are happy babies running all over the place."

I used to feel a heaviness in my heart when I would look at that photo. Tears would fill my eyes and a lump would form in my throat. Not anymore. Now when I look at the photo I hear the twins running up and down the hallway. When the twins died, I thought all our dreams died too. That dream didn't die at all. We just needed Poppy to show us our dream was alive and fulfilled.

Now, conversations about the presence of the twins and other deceased loved ones are a regular occurrence in our home. Poppy also speaks of Daisy, her guardian angel, and Archangel Michael. Poppy trusts Archangel Michael and puts on his blue bubble of protection each morning before school.

A few years later, my sister-in-law, Annette, passed unexpectedly from breast cancer. Poppy was only three, so I was torn over whether or not to take her to the funeral. In the end I decided to take her because of her relationship with her brother and sister. I believed she understood life and death enough to come to the funeral.

Five minutes into the service I was already regretting my decision. I just wished she would sit still. Poppy turned around in the church pew and began making faces at the couple sitting behind us. I scooped Poppy up and headed out of the sanctuary.

Poppy paced at the entrance to the sanctuary. She was more antsy than usual, talking nonstop and running from one place to another. Several older women were sitting together talking, and one of them raised a finger to her mouth and let out a loud *"Shhh!"* I was frustrated and not sure what to do with my active child. It was too cold to go outside, but finally I remembered the fellowship hall where everyone gathered after services. I opened the doors hoping to find it empty, but there were several women putting out food and drinks. I ushered Poppy inside anyway.

Poppy saw the stage in the front of the room and headed for it. She stood in the middle, quiet finally. After a few minutes, Poppy stepped off the stage and asked me for her special blanket. Then she returned to the stage and laid out her blanket in the middle, careful to smooth out every wrinkle. She stood on it, quiet again.

Poppy made two more trips from me to her blanket. She gathered a pink rose we brought from Annette's graveside service and Annette's memorial program that featured her photo on the front. Poppy carefully placed the rose and the program on her blanket and then stood on her blanket, raised her arms out to her sides, and twirled around.

"It's still not right."

Poppy came to me.

"Mommy, can I get into your purse?"

"Sure, what are you looking for?"

"The angels, Mommy, I need the angels."

Poppy rummaged through my purse and took out a card deck I carry that tells about seven archangels. She ran back to the stage and placed the angel card deck next to the other items she had gathered.

"Perfect!" Poppy declared.

Poppy began singing and dancing around her memorial to Annette. Her movements were slow and intentional. Her face was bright and a smile rested on her lips. She did pirouettes while holding her hands out gracefully. Her antsy vibration was gone and she embodied a sense of peace, love, and grace. She sang of Aunt Annette being there with all of us. She sang of love. She sang of presence. In this room with my daughter we celebrated Annette. There were no tears, only dancing and joy.

Poppy has noticed her father in the depths of grief and said, "But Mommy, he doesn't have to be sad. My brother, my sister, my grandma, my grandpa, and Aunt Annette are with us all the time." She closes her eyes tightly and says, "Just tell him to think about them really hard."

Often I hear people discount the thoughts and feelings of children. When I tell people about Poppy, they will often say, "Oh, she is just making it up!" I know better. She knows too much. She's shared too many facts to have made it up.

Poppy is my greatest teacher, especially when it comes to death. Through her I know that love and connection continue after death. The bond with our loved ones doesn't cease to exist upon death, it transforms. Poppy has shown me how to have a relationship with my twins.

Heaven touches the earth every day. We need only be open to the love present and available to us. In my case, the signs of love first came from my young daughter. After she showed me the way, I was able to open my heart and receive love directly from heaven. Sometimes the love is a feeling, and sometimes it comes as two butter-flies gliding on the wind or two feathers lying side by side on the grass. The love comes when I am in my heart and out of my head. My darling twins touch me from heaven every day.

～ 10 ～

The Documentary

Ellen Cooper

Rarely, someone or something has connected and reso-
nated with me so profoundly that the effects were lasting
and undeniable. This unique phenomenon seems to happen when and where it's least expected, yet most needed.
In this case, it was a documentary I watched about a singer
named Chely Wright. By the end of the documentary, I
felt moved and inspired in three ways. First was the way
this woman and her story represented me and my life; it
conveyed volumes about my own experiences. Second,
I felt a surge of creativity that I had not experienced in
a very long time. Third, and most importantly, I wanted
to emulate Chely Wright and her bravery by telling my
own story. By candidly sharing her experiences, Chely
was helping people. This was what I had wanted to do
for many years, by writing a book about my experiences
with adoption.

My mother, my sister Claire, and I were going to New
York City for a vacation. A few days prior to our trip,
I was telling some friends about our plans when one of
them asked, "If you could do absolutely anything while
you're in New York, what would you do?"

Without hesitation, I said "Chely Wright; I'd meet Chely Wright." Later, they wished me a wonderful trip and jokingly told me to say hello to Chely. I thanked my friends, laughed, and announced, "Of course I will! I am going to meet Chely Wright on my trip and I'll tell you all about it when I get back!"

Our joking exchange prompted me to think about the possibility, and I decided that it wouldn't hurt to "put it out in the universe." I sent a quick Twitter message to Chely that I wanted to meet her even though I knew there was little chance of her seeing the tweet and virtually no chance of actually meeting. But I felt compelled to do it anyway.

Once in New York, I thought about the possibility of running into Chely Wright. I knew it was utterly ridiculous! There are millions of people in the city, and it was statistically impossible for me to randomly encounter this one particular person. Why did I believe it would happen? *Don't waste your time and attention seeking something that isn't there*, I told myself. It made no sense to me that I had this expectation. I reminded myself several times to quit wasting my time and attention and to focus on what was actually happening! So, to the best of my ability, I released the notion.

Later that same evening, my sister, my mom, and I returned to our hotel after dinner. When we entered the lobby, a group was waiting to get on the next elevator. My attention was focused on a familiar man standing amid the group. I was desperately racking my brain, trying to remember how I knew the man. I thought maybe he was famous. Was he a newscaster? But when I pointed him out to Claire and asked her who he was, she didn't know. I had to hurry and remember because there was little to no chance that we would all fit on the elevator together. But thankfully, when the man got on the elevator with the others, a lady with a dog hesitated and gestured for us to go ahead of her. Yes! Now standing next to him, I felt rushed and almost panicked as the time dwindled with each passing floor. How did I know him? What should I say?

I had to find out who he was even though I was risking embarrassing myself in front of an elevator full of people.

"Excuse me, but how do I know you?" I asked as politely as possible.

His response sounded somewhat sarcastic: "I don't know; how do you know me?" I felt silly and embarrassed, but I also felt determined.

"I know you somehow. I just can't remember where I've seen you." I persisted.

"I've done interviews for CNN and MSNBC. That was probably it," he replied, watching the elevator button light up as it came to his floor. His companions were stepping off the elevator when I suddenly remembered.

"Were you in Chely Wright's documentary?"

"Yes, I was."

"Oh my God, I love you!" I literally and exuberantly replied. In a shocked and manic state, I began telling him about what I'd said when asked what I most wanted to do on my trip.

"When I told them I was coming up to New York, my friends asked what I would want to do most, and I said I wanted to meet Chely Wright! That documentary meant so much to me, and I am stunned that I ran into you here!" He smiled, and despite his initial sarcastic reply he seemed to warm to my enthusiasm.

His name was Welton Gaddy, and he was Chely Wright's friend and spiritual advisor. He was featured in the film and had greatly inspired and impressed me. The next thing I knew, I was sitting in Welton's family's hotel suite with him, his wife Judy, and their son John Paul.

It turned out they actually lived close to where I was from in Louisiana; and Welton even knew my late father! They had been friends and colleagues, as they were both clergy in the same part of the state. Welton was even familiar with a medical ministry started by my father, which had been dedicated to me and my sister, our names and credentials painted on the side of the mobile clinic.

I told Welton and his family about my aspiration to write a book, and we had such a warm and friendly conversation that I felt as though I had known them for years. Judy informed me that they were in town to attend a dinner the following night, where Welton was to receive an award. Most importantly, they told me that Chely would be there and I could purchase a ticket and attend the event. We exchanged contact information and made plans to be in touch the following evening.

The night of the award ceremony, I felt alone and nervous. Despite my nerves, I entered the venue and was given a warm welcome by Welton. Soon thereafter, Welton's family came up to me, including Judy, his sons John Paul and James, and their daughter-in-law Amanda. They were kind, welcoming, and enthusiastic about my being there. They were almost as amazed by the sequence of events that had occurred as I was.

Later that night, Welton took me under one arm and Chely under the other and brought us together. He told

Chely the story of how her film had impacted me and the sequence of events that had brought me there that evening. Chely held my hands as tears formed in her eyes. We hugged, took pictures, and chatted until the event was back under way with speeches and award presentations.

The synchronicity was astounding. No statistician could deny the virtual impossibility of the incalculable number and sequence of events that had to occur in order for this to have taken place.

After returning from my trip, I met with the friends to whom I laughingly said I would meet Chely Wright. And I told them the story. It was such a joy to tell them and others what had happened and to witness their reactions.

The true impact of this ceased to be about Chely Wright or the documentary and became something all its own. For so long my spiritual journey has consisted of seeking proof that there exists, in all of us, an eternal soul; that our lives mean more than we can fathom. But through this synchronistic event, I found that time and time again answers *have* been sent my way. I have learned to pay attention to even the small things when I ask for guidance and to simply be open to the gifts that are laid out for me. Sometimes it seems that when I stop looking so hard, that's when it happens. I've learned that following my gut/intuition will lead me toward what is being created for me by God, the universe, the interconnectedness of all, just as it did when so many small events aligned to bring me together with Chely Wright.

It was impossible that I would meet her in a city with over eight million inhabitants when I was only there for a few days. But the impossible *did happen* because I asked for it to be so and God and the universe provided. It was and is a gift that I not only treasure but also take tremendous joy in sharing. I know in my heart that this was a miracle, an answer to all of my prayers for a sign or proof. I have that proof now, and I know that miracles do happen, every day.

⇒ 11 ⇒

A Mother's Gift

Kathy Jackson

There are moments in time when we're walking through a tumultuous life event, unaware of how our future is about to change. Such was my experience in the early fall many years ago. It started when my partner got the phone call no daughter ever wants to receive, letting her know that her mom had choked while eating lunch and was in the ICU. As it turned out, that lunch was the last solid food her mom ever ate, and that day was the last day she ever spoke words. It was determined that she had late stage ALS (Lou Gehrig's disease).

The prognosis was not good. Nola would remain bed-ridden and on a respirator for her final few months. Life dramatically changed for all of us that day. My partner, Casey, began spending every moment of her free time at the hospital with Nola. Their relationship had been strained throughout most of Casey's life, but now a new kind of bond was forming between them. Nola loved having her hair brushed and lotion rubbed on her hands and feet. She loved listening to music, especially her favorite song, "Amazing Grace." She was physically dying, yet she had full cognitive awareness. As Casey read Kahlil Gibran's *The Prophet* to her mother, I enjoyed witnessing the love between them slowly deepening. Nola was finally, truly getting to know her daughter.

The sunny afternoon when Nola took her final breath was both sad and joyous. Nola's spirit had at last been freed from the tomb of her body. As I stood in the hospital hallway to give Casey a few moments alone with her mom, I heard a familiar melody—"Amazing Grace," the song that had brought Nola so much comfort in her final weeks. The friend who was visiting that day heard it as well. We looked at each other in curiosity, wondering where the music was coming from.

We wandered down the corridor, poking our heads into each room's doorway to see if we could determine the source. The song was hard to trace because it seemed to float ahead of us and behind us, in equal measure, no matter where we wandered. We combed the entire hospital floor and still came up with no reasonable explanation. Nowhere had we found a room or source from which the song would have logically originated. We looked at each other in wonderment. Could it really be? We both knew the answer: Yes! Yes, it was a message from Nola. A message saying, "Farewell, thank you, and I'm okay." It was the final hug, wrapped in a song.

Even though I'd barely known Nola prior to her illness, I felt an incredible bond had formed between us during those hospital visits. So much so that even many months later, long after Casey and I had ended our relationship, I continued to feel Nola's presence in my life. In the year following Nola's death I went through a tremendous spiritual and energetic shift. Physically, I felt like I was attached to a battery jumper cable. I felt as though

I were walking through a thick fog, unable to sleep, eat, or sit still for more than five minutes. Emotionally, I was hungry. I read many spiritually nourishing books and vowed to stay open to feeling everything I needed to feel in order to heal and grow.

During this time I found walking to be especially beneficial to my emotional well-being. It was during these tree-lined, surreal walks, where the road meets the grass, that I heard it again. Nola's song, "Amazing Grace." I heard it as clearly as I heard the birds. Each time the song started to play, the hair on my neck, right arm, and right leg would stand on end, and a single tear would flow from the outer corner of my right eye. I knew beyond any doubt that it was Nola reaching out to me in my time of need, just as I had reached out to her in hers. She was using her signature song to communicate the same message she had shared the day she transitioned—the message that everything was okay.

Months passed, and I grew emotionally stronger day by day. I felt Nola's calming presence around me always, yet one particular day it was more vivid than ever. I was driving, and I had the distinct feeling Nola was leading me somewhere. Once I decided to surrender to the directions I was intuitively receiving from my old friend, I found myself at Penn Square Mall. I am not a shopper! A shopping mall is the last place on earth anyone would ever find me. But there I was with a knowing inside that I was on a mission.

As I walked through the mall trying to feel into Nola's guidance and its purpose, I was led into a little safari-themed store with earth games, fountains, and all types of jungle animals, from plastic to stuffed. It was probably the only store in the mall I would actually enjoy.

I browsed curiously through the items on display. There was nothing I needed or wanted, yet I knew I was there for a reason. Finally I reached the wall with the water fountains, where I stood still for several minutes, asking to understand what Nola was trying to share with me. I was engulfed by the familiar sensation of the hair on my neck and right side standing on end, and a single tear flowing from the outer corner of my right eye.

That's when the message landed in my consciousness. Casey's birthday was the following week, and Nola wanted to give her daughter a birthday present. I scanned the fountains, seemingly through Nola's eyes, until my gaze fell on a beautiful fountain with a family of wolves on a mountainside. The water flowed down over the rocks and around the wolf pack, delivering a soothing message of family. This was the reason I was here.

I looked at the price and gulped. It was more than I could afford. I said, "If this fountain turns out to be on sale and I can buy it for under $100, I'll know this is what I'm supposed to get." I took the boxed unit to the register, and sure enough, it went home with me. But here's the thing about getting a birthday present for your ex-partner from her deceased mother—it seems kind of crazy. After much internal debate I was finally able to move beyond my sense of how this would look or feel to the recipient. I simply had to trust in the truth of the message I was receiving from Nola. I had to deliver this gift from a mother to her daughter. Nola had entrusted me with her wish and led me to take the steps to fulfill it. I wasn't going to let her down.

My life has taken many twists and turns over the last fifteen years since that pivotal moment in the hospital when I first made a true connection with the other side.

Though my experiences have been many, and my ability to sense and acknowledge has continued to increase, one of the sweetest parts of my ongoing spiritual journey is still the occasional reoccurrence of "Amazing Grace" and a single tear.

❧ 12 ❧

POP! Goes the Dryer

Janet Rozzi

Laughter, pizza, hunting, and tile craftsmanship—that is how I will forever remember my Uncle Ray, and pretty much in that order. I adored my Uncle Ray. His laughter was boisterous, and he had an endless amount of energy. He could whip up a pizza from scratch, seemingly at a moment's notice, and his special ingredient was love. Being around him simply made you feel good. He had a passion for hunting, made very accessible with acres of Back Mountain hunting territory behind his home. He would hunt with his four sons and his loyal dog by his side. He was a tile contractor by trade, and he knew the value and pride of extremely hard work.

People like him should live forever. Their joy is pure energy, and their positivity is infectious. Time spent with them is never long enough, and they always leave us wanting more.

One dreary early December day a few years ago, I received a call from my parents that my Uncle Ray had suddenly passed away. I was profoundly saddened by the news, and to be honest, I felt a bit cheated of time with him. I wanted to close my eyes and have it be a dream, to know that all would be okay and that he was still with us when I awoke. But when I opened my eyes, it was still true.

On the morning of the funeral, I was getting ready and my uncle was deeply on my mind. I was sifting through all of my favorite memories with him, wishing I could have had just a little bit more time with him, if for no other reason than to tell him how much I loved him and to share with him exactly how much he meant to me. I was blow-drying my hair when I thought to myself, *I wonder if you can show me a sign that you are still with me, Uncle Ray.*

Within two seconds, there was a loud *POP!* and the blow-dryer stopped working. It stunned me, and I almost dropped the blow-dryer! Then I immediately heard my uncle's timeless chuckle, his words, *Ah, I'm just joshing you!*, and another chuckle. I hadn't heard these words from him in almost twenty years! I burst forth a laugh, and smiled. I was so happy to hear his voice once again, and to know he was still around, but I was also a little unnerved by how quickly I saw evidence of him still being with me even after he'd passed. I was hesitant to see what else might happen if I asked for more evidence of his presence. Albeit amazing, I wasn't sure I was ready for more direct interaction with his spirit at that time. So I grabbed another blow-dryer, determined to focus on getting ready for the funeral and not ask my uncle for anything else while I was doing so.

I went to the funeral with the peace of mind that my uncle was in a better place, and that he was still the happy-go-lucky uncle I always knew. Nothing had changed. He had labored hard at his job, and always worked so hard to cater to his wife of fifty years and his family, and I knew that even now he was still carrying out that duty by being with them. Initially I was sad that he did not get to fully enjoy the years of relaxation that retirement can bring, but he seemed to be just as happy on the other side, as evidenced by the little prank he'd played on me. I knew it was a sign that he was okay, and happy, and still with those who loved him, even though his physical body was being laid to rest.

The funeral was packed with family, friends, and neighbors whose lives he'd touched. I thought it was a little ironic how much sadness there was for a man who had inspired so much laughter. I half pictured him trying to make a joke to lighten the situation, as was always his gift.

While at the family luncheon, post funeral services, my cousin shared with me that just a few months earlier my uncle had "hung up" his guns and officially retired from his lifelong hunting hobby. It seemed a sudden yet definitive decision. My uncle shared that it was his last hunting excursion, and perhaps he also knew that it was his last Father's Day; he would not see another. It's almost as if he knew when the end was near, and that he would make his transition soon. He never mentioned anything else to the family about whether or not he knew that he would transition, but I have heard similar stories of people who seem to know when their moment is coming and make synchronistic plans, just as my uncle had.

As much as my experience with my uncle's spirit scared me a little at first, I have opened myself up to the possibility of what lies beyond our three-dimensional world, and I feel comforted that our loved ones remain with us after they have shed their human bodies. It was a small miracle for me to see truly how we can have our loved ones stay with us in our hearts and in our own spirit (and sometimes even interact with us!). With practice, I am now used to listening to divine guidance, the soft inner voice that whispers to me when I need assurance or direction on which way to go. If I am still and quiet, without being distracted by everything around me, I am able to hear the guidance. I no longer ask deceased loved ones to show me they're present with me (because on some level I understand that I am still not quite ready for that!), but I do ask that they stay close to me, particularly when they feel that I may need to have love surrounding me.

I have asked for divine guidance in other areas of my life, too. If it can help me on a deeper level with life's big questions, then why not tap into this resource for every-day guidance as well? Some of my questions are big and some are smaller: Are our loved ones still with us after they transition from human being to pure spirit? Which way do I go on this road? Where did I leave my keys? When I have these questions, I know that if I remain still enough I can hear my inner voice that whispers, *Take the road to the right*; and *Check the refrigerator for your keys*. The challenge is to remember to stay quiet in order to hear my inner voice and not allow the inner chatter to interfere.

With a loud *POP!* and my uncle's simple words on the morning of his funeral, my world opened up in a whole new way. I now understand that this gift of a life is much richer than we can ever imagine. If only we have the courage to explore, get out of our comfort zone a bit, and be open to possibility. It may seem subtle, but my uncle spoke to me in a way that let me fully understand that it was him. Perhaps subtle was what I needed at the time, until I could become more comfortable receiving such messages.

Now I enjoy tapping into divine guidance on a regular basis to help experience life to its fullest. I have a better understanding of life's big questions (such as what happens to us when leave here), but more importantly, it has helped me get still and quiet so I can pay attention and fully appreciate each day, and enjoy the extraordinary memories that are created in what seems like ordinary everyday life. And when I feel I need a bit of support, hope, and comfort, I know that I am not limited to loved ones who are still here with me, and that love truly knows no boundaries.

⟣ 13 ⟢

Undying Friendship

Michelle McDonald Vlastnik

I was in kindergarten and hanging upside down on the monkey bars, struggling to hold my dress in place when my legs let go. I was not hurt, but I did cry a little. My teacher sat me at a table to rest. That is when Randy came over to cheer me up and we became inseparable best friends.

Randy Parker, the blond, green-eyed boy with the raspy voice, happened to be the boy next door, living kitty-corner across the road from me. We were carefree kids just having fun—riding in the wagon behind his dad's lawn mower, shooting mice in the barn, drinking pop through pixie sticks, eating Hot Tamale candies while we sat on the tailgate of his dad's old truck, and riding our bikes over homemade ramps. Kindred spirits, that is what we were, and I loved hanging out with him!

It was a warm summer day in August 1972. I was nine years old. A bunch of us kids got together to play an innocent game of hospital. The two boys were admitted because one had hit the other on his motorcycle. We used Smarties for pills and candy bars for meals. These were a child's cure for all illness. Well, the game grew long, and patients grew tired of the pretend play. To end his role in the game, Randy said, "Just pretend I died." Little did I know how eerily haunting this game would become as part of my memory of this day.

Later that same evening, Randy stopped by my house to see if I wanted to go bike riding. My little cousin and sister wanted to tag along. I placed my cousin in front of me on the banana bike seat so I could hold on to him during the ride and my little sister hopped on the back of Randy's bike seat. At the last minute, I decided that my little cousin should stay home, and I told my sister to ride with me. The significance of this decision would be life changing in the moments to come.

We headed up the country road with my sister's dog running in the field alongside of Randy who rode on the berm. Randy was on one side of the road, and I was on the other. Almost to our turnoff, I could hear a motorcycle whining in the distance, and I moved from the berm to the field. Randy was crossing the road to join me when suddenly the motorcycle rounded the blind curve, hugging the center line.

Impact!

The force was so great it stopped the motorcycle instantaneously. My friend was launched right out of one of his socks and shoes, lifted into the air over the telephone wires, landing in the field right in front of my bike. The sound of the wind being knocked from his body as he hit the ground was unforgettable.

I slammed on my bike brakes to avoid hitting him! Horrified, I jumped off my bike and started to run home for help. Oh my gosh, my sister! She had been on the back of my bike. Where is Vanessa? I turned back to look for her. She was staring, paralyzed by his motionless body. Pulling her arm, I yelled, "Come on, Vanessa!" I began once again to run home for help. Everything was moving in slow motion with fog etching the corners of my view. Nothing felt real. I could see the people coming out from inside their houses. I could hear my voice screaming the words, "Randy got hit! Randy got hit by a motorcycle!"

The ambulance and the police arrived on the scene. There was a police car parked in the field halfway between my house and where the ambulance was. I was being told that the police wanted to talk to me, but I did not want to go where my friend lay. My God! I did not want to see my best friend hurt like that. I did not want that memory! I was leaning back, resisting, as I was pushed toward the police car. I saw the paramedics lift my friend and place him on the gurney, his leg dangling by a strip of flesh.

I was a very scared little girl, obviously still in shock from my traumatic experience, and now I found myself sitting in the front seat of a police car. The voice of the policeman, asking his questions, was a distant muffle in my ears as I looked down at my blood-spattered legs and flicked a piece of my friend's skin off my knee and watched it stick to the car dash. I knew in my heart that my friend would die. Didn't anyone care?

That evening the house felt somber. Both my parents had been called home from work. I began running my bathwater and then went to tell my mom what was on my heart. She was at the sink washing dishes. I asked her if we could go to Randy's funeral because I knew that he was going to die. She said yes. I went into the bathroom and took a bath, scrubbing every inch of my legs.

The following day we got the news that my friend had died.

Sometime between his death and his funeral, Randy came to visit me. It was like a dream, but different. It was a place in space, maybe like a starless night, and then Randy was standing right in front of me. I was so excited and happy to see him! He looked so much older wearing that suit. I had never seen him dressed up that way. Heck, he had always worn play clothes—cutoff shorts, a striped T-shirt—and usually he was barefoot. This night he had on a dark suit with a white dress shirt, a striped tie, and he was not wearing any shoes. He just had on a pair of white tube socks.

He told me that he had to find his way back to me because he wanted to make sure that I was all right and he wanted to say good-bye. I was so happy to see him! I loved my friend so very much. The visit was too short. *Don't go, Randy! Please, stay a little longer.* I woke up crying.

My spirit felt broken and my heart ached. My mom held my hand as we walked up to Randy's casket at the funeral parlor. He looked like he was sixteen years old even though he was only nine. Just like in my dream, he wore a dark suit with a white dress shirt and a striped tie. I looked down toward his feet, but the lower half of the casket was closed so I could not see what kind of shoes they had put on him. I stood there for a while, just missing my friend, wondering, will my heart ever stop hurting?

I saw his parents in the front row. Mr. Parker was a big, tall man, but today he was hunched over and sobbing as Mrs. Parker hugged him. I wanted so much to go over and hug him too. His pain was deeply felt, and my heart ached for him.

The week after the funeral I took my purple Huffy bike into the house and stood at the top of the basement stairs and let go. I watched it bump down the wooden steps and crash at the bottom. Then I closed the basement door and locked it.

It took me about a week to muster up enough courage to ask Randy's sister what kind of shoes they had buried him in. I did not want to make her feel any sadder, but I really needed to know if he was actually just wearing white tube socks, as I had envisioned. She said that he had been. Everything matched exactly how I had seen him when he came back to make sure that I was okay and to say good-bye. It turned out that this would not be the only time Randy would appear to me.

Sometime after Randy's death, I was sitting in my dad's recliner watching television when I saw someone riding a bike in front of our house. It was Randy, plain as day, riding his bike on the road. I jumped up and went to the giant picture window to see him. I watched him turn, ride into our driveway, and disappear halfway up to the house. I was ecstatic and ran to tell my mom, who insisted that I had been dreaming. But I knew, as I have known since I was three years old and first began to see spirits, that it was Randy, coming to visit me as he had so often in life.

Randy even came to me through a song, called *Seasons in the Sun*, by Terry Jacks. Even today it touches my soul when I hear it, knowing that it came from my friend.

Pure joy is what my soul felt whenever I was around my friend. Even after his death, he has been my greatest teacher. He showed me unconditional love and honored every aspect of my being. I know what having a free spirit feels like because of him. That feeling has been my compass throughout my life's journey, leading me to the rediscovery of my Authentic Self. I am grateful for the four years that I got to spend here on earth with this shining Being of Light. I am excited that recently Randy has become one of my spiritual guides as I continue fulfilling my Life Purpose mission by helping others rediscover their Authentic Self. I will forever hold him in my heart because he has proven to me that death is only the end of the body. The soul is eternal.

⌒ 14 ⌒

The Spirit of Cancer

Jodie Harvala

We heard the news: my mother-in-law Priscilla had stage four pancreatic cancer. Terminal. Not more than a few weeks later, we received a call from a friend, Loren—he had been diagnosed with stage four throat and liver cancer, also terminal. Then my good friend Beth contacted me with even more news: breast cancer.

These three diagnoses came within weeks of each other. I felt crushed. Every night I lay awake, trying to discern what all of this meant.

The phrase "lose two, one lives" came to me from seemingly nowhere. I heard this message over and over in my head. As a psychic-medium, I could feel that this was going to be the true outcome, whether I wanted it or not. Honestly, it just pissed me off to feel as though the universe was giving me this message just to take away the hope that I had. I could feel in my spirit that my mother-in-law and Loren would both die of their cancers. I also knew that Beth would suffer but she would live through it.

I began having panic attacks. My chest would tighten up and no breath would come into my body. My thoughts would spin and spin on what this all meant. I had been afraid of death my entire life, and now three people close to me were on the edge of life? Little did I know that Spirit had a plan to ease my pain.

As I traversed this journey with these three people, I was grateful to have a strong mentor who reminded me to be present in each moment, and to look for the gifts of what was happening. I took her advice to heart and began to mindfully practice living in the moment with my dear friends and family.

My mother-in-law was a badass in her cancer journey. She outlived every "expiration date" the doctors threw at her. Though she had only been given four months to live, I swear that she looked at us, at her family, and thought to herself, "Nope—these people still need me." Seventeen months later, she took her last breath.

My friend Loren held so much hope that he was going to beat cancer. I held that space with him until I knew it was time. Loren knew as well, because he wrote me a message in response to a friendly request I'd sent him, joking about how we would have a secret word so that I'd have a clear sign that his spirit was with me. I'd decided on "Disneyland" as our code word; but Loren's reply simply read, "Love you." As it turned out, he had sent those words, those messages of unconditional love, out to many of his friends and family members through e-mail and voice mail or Facebook pages. To this day, many of us still have them saved so that we have a daily reminder of his love even after his passing.

Beth, on the other hand, stayed incredibly private but would check in once in a while and tell me the most amazing stories about what she had felt or seen or experienced in moments when she felt as though she was disconnected from the world. Her suffering during her breast cancer treatments was intense, but Beth came from it with lessons and messages straight from Spirit. Each moment of physical agony opened her heart and her mind to Spirit, and she swears by how this experience with cancer, difficult as it was, changed her life immensely.

Loren passed away first. It was July, and I knew he would die at some point that week. Unprompted, I woke up in the middle of the night and sat straight up in bed. I heard someone shout *I'm here!* very clearly.

In my sleepy state I thought, "Who is here, and why are you in my house at three in the morning?"

As I pushed myself up to get out of bed and see who had arrived, I distinctly heard someone say, *No, it's time to go back to sleep.* Gently, someone guided me back to my pillow, and I immediately fell into a deep, restful sleep. At six o'clock I woke again with a sense of urgency. I sat up fast out of a solid sleep and grabbed my phone. I saw the text. Loren had passed away in the night. I knew Loren had come to me in the night to show me that he was going where he needed to be, and though I cried and grieved, the fact that I knew he was safe and at peace brought me and my family the greatest comfort.

Even the next day I continued to receive signs from Loren—in the form of Disneyland commercials that seemed to play endlessly, as though Loren were there saying, *Do you see? Do you see what I'm sending you?* I laughed and said aloud, "I hear you!" He was still with us; and I knew that he would be helping my mother-in-law as she also made her transition.

Thirteen months after her original "expiration date," Priscilla was beginning to fade. I could feel my beloved mother-in-law's spirit popping in and out of her body as she neared death, and I felt her visit me in these times. Her spirit was driven by unconditional love for her family and her strong faith and love for God.

One night I felt a presence in my room. Even though I am a psychic-medium, I still don't care for the late-night visits, as they can feel somewhat spooky. Thinking this was Priscilla making her transition, I tuned in to the energy—but it didn't feel comforting and warm, like her. I said aloud, "I don't know who you are, but get out." The spirit left, and I returned to sleep.

But the next night, the strange entity returned. Again, I told it to leave, that I had no idea who it was and was uncomfortable with its presence. Again, it left.

When the entity returned a third time, I reached out to a friend who was a fellow psychic-medium for advice. What she told me shook me to my core.

"It's the spirit of cancer. She wants to talk to you. Ask her what she is teaching you."

She had to be freaking kidding me! Priscilla was getting worse, and I was getting angry. I had no interest in talking to the damn spirit of cancer, unless it was to give it a piece of my mind!

For the forth night in a row, the spirit appeared to me. This time, I took a deep breath and settled myself for a conversation.

"What do you want to teach me?" I asked, trying to hold back my anger and annoyance. This spirit looked like my mother-in-law but sick and dark and sad, as though she were wearing a gray veil or was somehow hidden. I'll admit it was spooky, and I was more than a little scared by her appearance. All of a sudden, the veil began to peel away, layer by layer. I felt more than heard her when she told me that each layer represented all the emotions we have about cancer. We hate it, we resent it, we want to kill it, we want to control it—all those ugly things come up when cancer shows itself to us. As she finished pulling away the veil, I saw something fascinating beneath. The center of cancer—the center of the spirit that showed up that night—was pure love.

I didn't understand. Pure love. I asked this spirit to show me an explanation of how it could be pure love. These memories started pouring through my mind of the last year, the battles that we had fought with Loren, Priscilla, and Beth. The spirit showed me the laughs, the hugs, the honest talks, and the hand-holding between us. The spirit showed me how my mother-in-law's illness brought about life changes through the entire family. I saw her husband standing at her side each minute, making sure she was comfortable and taken care of. I saw my own personal growth as I learned how to show up and be present even in my fear of death, finding out I had a choice about how I walked through it. Watching my husband hold his mom's hand while she got weaker and weaker still stings my eyes because of how soft and vulnerable he was in those moments. It was pure love, and we had the opportunity and the honor of walking that path with her. We still had the anger and the resentment and the fear—but beneath it all, at the very center, was *pure love*. This perspective was one that I had never expected.

After that experience something inside me shifted. I could see the gifts of cancer so much more clearly than I had before. I still felt a little anger, and grieved, of course—but I also had an understanding that this experience was meant to change our lives. It was a gift.

I stayed home with the kids the day that Priscilla passed. An overwhelming tiredness washed over me, and I was napping when I was woken by sirens and bells and whistles. My husband called soon after to tell me his mother had died. I do believe she was telling me with those loud whistles and horns that she had arrived as well! That night, as I went to sleep, I had a vision of her walking up a rainbow bridge where Loren waited, holding out his hand to assist her and bring her into the crowd of loved ones who had passed before her. I also heard him say, "It's okay. I have her." And I knew he did. I saw her walk into that light and love and knew she was at peace.

And though it was a rough journey, thanks to the Spirit of Cancer, I feel at peace as well, knowing that at the center of all our pain and strife lies a core of pure love waiting to be revealed.

The Miracle of Marc

Jean Mulvihill

When my youngest son Daniel came into our lives twenty-three years ago, inexplicable things began to happen. Ghosts frequented our home, negative energy came in and out, and unexplainable occurrences became the norm for our family. Daniel, we discovered, has some amazing spiritual gifts. He can see, hear, and feel spirits and ghostly entities that have been with him both spiritually and physically since he was born.

As an infant, Daniel had constant ear infections. At five years old, he developed a terminal kidney disease that mysteriously went into remission after only a few months. And as an adolescent, he had heart issues that couldn't be diagnosed.

Daniel then developed stomach issues as a teenager. There were days he couldn't eat without throwing up. The episodes would last only a day or so, and then he would be magically better. This cycle continued for years. Again, with no medical diagnosis.

What we discovered was that spirit energy is attracted to him, and when a negative energy attaches to him, he gets sick—sometimes dangerously so.

Daniel's stomach issues continued for years, but one particular time it was exceptionally severe. He was lying in bed, looking like the poster child for the commercials asking for aid to a poor country. He was so skinny and pale. My heart broke as I saw the energy he was expending just to open his eyes and speak. He hadn't eaten in seven days. I prayed to God and anyone else who could hear to please help my son, but no one seemed to be listening!

I was watching my twenty-three-year-old baby die from starvation, and no one was doing anything to help him. There must be someone somewhere who can help him, I thought. There just had to be. We couldn't just stand by and watch him die. Who do you go to for help with negative entities and energies?

I phoned Jane, my best friend in the whole world, for comfort and possibly some answers. We'd been in contact almost daily since this spiritual journey started. She's very patient and listens to my concerns, even through tears. But this time, she was also at a loss for an answer. She suggested that we search for spiritual churches that might be able to help us.

The reaction I received from the first church threw me off balance: "Negative energy? Oh no, we don't deal with anything from the 'dark' side. We don't deal with anything negative. We don't deal with spiritual mediums."

I decided there was no reason to phone the others.

The tears wouldn't stop, and I was exhausted from worry. On my drive home, I spoke through tears to my deceased mother—as I have many times over the past few years. "Please help him," I said. "Please help me. Why isn't there anyone that can help him? I don't know what to do. Please guide me. Please don't let my son die."

I rambled on and on, selfishly making demands and asking for help in my desperation to save my son and wondering why no answers had come.

While I was desperately praying to my mother and anyone else who might be listening (but choosing not to grant my prayers), that same evening Jane was sitting in her home at her computer searching online for spiritual counseling or psychic mediums who might be able to help us. She got up to grab some water, picked up her phone, and accidentally swiped it. Before she knew it, somehow, her phone was calling Marc, a psychic she'd met through her work nearly eighteen years before. She wouldn't even have had his phone number if they hadn't miraculously reestablished contact only a few months prior, when he came looking for her at her work, hoping to rekindle their lost friendship.

Thinking it must have been a "butt dial," or simply an accidental flick of the finger over her contacts list, Jane was absolutely shocked to find that she was calling Marc. She scrambled to hang up, but it was too late.

"Hello?" Marc answered.

Embarrassed, Jane made small talk with him, trying to pretend that she had called him on purpose so as not to be rude. As they chatted, she thought of Daniel, whom she had been trying to find help for all evening, only to end up on the phone with Marc accidentally. Or perhaps it was no accident at all . . .

Jane wasn't sure why, but she began to tell Marc about my son's predicament and explained his spiritual gifts. She conveyed that negative energy had influenced him so much that he could no longer eat, and she was worried.

There was a long, awkward silence before Marc replied to what Jane was sure he would think was an outlandish story.

"I may be able to help him," Marc said, and Jane's body was flooded with hope and relief. "I am listening to my spirit guides," Marc continued quietly, "and they are saying that we were brought together so that I could help him." Jane immediately gave Marc my contact information, and Marc and I set an appointment for a call with Daniel.

Just the next day, Daniel was feeling better and tried to eat some crackers. He was very weak, but at least he was eating. I was sure this was a sign of good things to come.

A few days later, Marc called Daniel and counseled him by phone. Marc and Daniel discussed their spiritual gifts, but more than that, Marc was able to mentor Daniel in a way that I couldn't have dreamed. He taught him techniques to keep negative entities out of his energy, while still accepting and allowing those from the light in. For a few days, Marc was Daniel's key teacher in how to manage his spiritual gifts—and lo and behold, Daniel started to recover.

The doctors couldn't explain yet another miraculous recovery for my son, but I know that it is because the universe brought Marc to us to teach Daniel how to control his gifts. Now, when Daniel feels sick, he has the tools to remove the negative energies that he is sensitive to. He still has much to learn about his new world, but he is happy and more confident with his gifts.

Just as I lost hope, the universe answered my prayers. The right person was sent to help Daniel at the right time. The universe is always sending us help and guidance in times of need. Though we were looking for someone to help Daniel, we never actually *found* Marc; he simply appeared when we needed him, the answer to our prayers.

I have learned that there is a reason for every person who crosses our path. There are no mistakes or coincidences. When we ask, we will receive an answer. You too may be called to be someone's miracle. The only way to know is to keep your heart open and to allow the universe to work and guide you toward your miraculous purpose.

≈ 16 ≈

Conversations with Max

Mandy Berlin

I'll never forget the miraculous New Year's Day when my beloved Max came to me—just nine days after he had died—forever shattering my agnostic tendencies and prior beliefs about death. I'd spent that miserable morning feeling sorry for my dear, sweet husband, taken so young by the ravages of cancer—and also feeling sorry for myself. Though I'd always known it would be hard after Max transitioned, I'd never imagined just *how* hard it would be. As I wallowed that morning in the memories and images from his funeral, still so fresh in my heart, I was shocked to hear a voice embedded in an unusual buzzing sound, almost as if it were arising from the back of my brain.

Shaken to the core, I let out a shriek. Something or someone was there! I could barely detect words beneath the surreal buzzing, like the sound of white noise. Trying to regain my composure, I turned toward the sound. "What?" I asked. "What are you saying?"

When I still couldn't decipher the syllables, I mustered the courage to yell, "Louder! I can't hear you!" I needed to know what those words were!

Then, all at once, like a blast from infinity, the words *socks up!* seemed to echo off the back of my neck. The masculine tenor was deep and felt close to my head, yet the pitch was strangely high. That's the best description I'm able to offer to anyone who has never experienced something so odd. It seemed the phrase "socks up" represented the tail end of a sentence I hadn't been able to fully make out. And although the resonance was higher than any normal sound I'd ever heard, it was still clear to me that the voice was Max's.

Even as I was flooded with joy at the contact from my deceased husband, my agnostic scientist's brain wrestled with the idea of white noise coming to me from another dimension. As a statistician for over twenty years, I knew it wasn't truly white noise at all. White noise has no pattern; yet this communication was definitely from some sort of entity capable of creating a detectable pattern that emerged in the form of a sentence. The unique sibilance of the words and overall familiarity of the tone left no doubt in my mind that it was Max. Or his soul. Or his something-or-other.

I leapt from my chair and stood straight up to signal my willingness to receive. Shaking, I turned in the direction of the voice and asked, "Socks up? What on earth are you trying to tell me, Max?"

Getting no response, I panicked, fearing the moment had passed and I'd missed the message. As loud as I could, I yelled, "Hey, I don't get it! Tell me more! I want to know!"

And then the voice was there again! Right at the back of my head, between my neck and my right ear. It said, *Pull your socks up, mate!*

I felt like I could go into shock. I plopped back down in my chair, afraid I'd pass out. Breathing deeply, I did all I could to collect myself and shift out of my state of helplessness. Whatever was going on here, I knew I did not want to miss it. I rubbed my neck and head until I felt more grounded, and then I turned to get up. But before I could rise from the chair, I heard Max again in my ear. *Hey, Luv, do you get it? Hmmm?*

Simultaneously, I saw a haze of white iridescence appear to my right. The shimmering beam of light was long and thin, as if it were being pulled through an infinitesimally small hole. Once through, it expanded, right there in my dining room, seemingly shape-shifting to adapt to my three-dimensional world. I would have been terrified if not for the familiar sight it created— Max in profile!

To this day, I don't know if my eyes were open or closed when I caught that glimpse of Max's phenomenal spirit. I believe they were open, but it was like observing a flared-out hologram. Was I actually viewing his presence, or was his image somehow being transmitted directly into my mind from some other location? I did not know then, and I do not know now.

Since that day, all I've known for sure is that Max spoke to me from the other side, lovingly chiding me for my devastation and delivering an inspirational message in his distinctly cheeky, Englishman style. I heard his voice. I saw his face, too.

It was his voice I found myself missing most of all one lonely evening a few months later. Praying had become a regular practice for me since that dining room experience, so on this particular evening I prayed with all my heart that I might hear Max's voice again.

The following day I flipped on the television and attempted to change the channel. Nothing happened.

Assuming the remote control needed new batteries, I went out to the garage to see what I could find. Batteries had been one of those things Max had always taken care of, so it took a bit of sleuthing to discover where he'd stashed the fresh ones. I finally discovered them in the hutch—a whole pack of double As.

I hadn't had any reason to open that hutch for a long time. So long that I'd forgotten what was in there. I picked up the pack of batteries and pulled out the ones I needed. But as I tossed the package back into the hutch, something caught my eye. It was the handheld personal recorder Max had always carried in his pocket! I smiled to myself, recalling how he liked to tape his project notes and other random thoughts while he sat in traffic. He had considered it the perfect way to make the most of those otherwise wasted hours.

I extracted the contraption from the random odds and ends, and was delighted to discover there was a tape inside. I took the tape player into the kitchen, set it up on the counter, turned the volume knob to full blast, and pressed Play. No sound. Nada. Maybe it's reading the end of the tape, I thought. So I rewound it to the beginning and pressed Play again.

Then I heard it. Like a small child who's just opened a Christmas gift, I jumped with a start. "It's Max!" I exclaimed, soaking up the familiar sound. I brushed back a tear, marveling at how perfectly Max's tone and character had been preserved on this little magnetic ribbon. The recording was made long ago, yet there I sat, listening as though he were right beside me talking to me, pouring out the contents of his brilliant mind. Bowled over, as always, by my husband's fascinating words and thoughts, I was powerless to keep the tears from my eyes. So I just let them flow.

I'd always been amazed at the nature and depth of Max's ideas. He had a tendency to think outside the box and to defy time-tested notions. He was forever catching people off guard, testing me, and sometimes even inciting me to riot. We had shared so many heated (yet fun and thought-provoking) debates. To this day I believe that one of Max's primary purposes here on earth was to challenge people, to open their eyes. Whoever sat down to dinner with Max went home digesting more than a meal—whether it was a new thought, a new feeling, a new insight, or perhaps even a totally different reality to ponder. I can truly say no one ever left our table indifferent.

Even after his death, he'd found a way to open my eyes about the whole afterlife business. And here he was again, challenging my worldview with his expansive perspectives. When the recording ended, I ejected the tape and told Max I'd keep it forever. I'd even make copies for our friends. I found a felt-tip pen and printed these words across the empty title line: *On Art and Life: The Philosophy of Max Blau.*

"Hey, guy, I hope you don't mind. I titled your tape."

Max never titled any of his work unless his employer requested it. He reviled titles, labels, and limitations of almost any kind, just as he despised the way people are often labeled. He even disliked borders or frames around works of art. Max was my hero.

As the last rays of a blazing sun reflected off the patio chimes and onto the living room rug, I sat cross-legged on the floor and replayed Max's tape again and again. It relaxed me to hear his calm voice and his amazing thoughts. I raised a wrinkled sleeve to wipe the salty crust from my face, and as day turned to dusk, I was struck by the enormity of what had occurred.

"Oh my God," I cried, arms outstretched toward the ceiling. "How did I not see? Last night I prayed to hear Max's voice, and in less than twenty-four hours, my prayer was answered!"

⟾ 17 ⟿

A Divinely Orchestrated "Accident"

Karen Hasselo

It was the spring of 1971. From outside appearances, my life looked as perfect as our beautifully manicured lawn. I was a junior high school student studying geometry and biology. I excelled at playing the clarinet in the concert band. I lived in a safe, affluent neighborhood. However, inside my home, filled with Persian rugs and exquisite antiques, all four of my family members were utterly estranged from one another.

Both of my parents were intellectually gifted and highly ethical people. Nevertheless, from the beginning of their relationship, they were emotionally and temperamentally mismatched. By 1971, they rarely wasted their energy on verbal combat. Instead, their war had morphed into a silent one. My parents had been emotionally absent for much of my life, stemming from their own fractured childhoods. Their absence was compounded by my father's escalating self-medication with alcohol. Because I viewed myself as a burden to the very people who were tasked with nurturing me, I looked for strategies to sublimate my pain.

I sought emotional first aid by avoiding my home life and immersing myself in extracurricular pursuits. In the year prior, my parents had blessed me with a large dappled gray thoroughbred Welsh pony. I found solace in my relationship with the horses at the stable and was intently focused on mastering the art of riding, irrespective of the fact that my instructor emotionally brutalized her students. My mother spent untold hours at the stable as an employee. However, she chose to look the other way when I was subjected to my instructor's rage attacks. Based upon my prior experiences with a number of adults, I had developed a cynical view of life and a self-protective distrust for authority figures.

In the aftermath of a breakup, the in-group at school had recently ostracized me. At the tender age of fourteen, I had already become disillusioned with the amount of effort required to earn a modicum of emotional support from adults as well as my peers. It was becoming increasingly difficult to muster the internal resources required to fulfill the role of overachiever, perfectionist, junior high school social climber, and workaholic. I did not know any other way to navigate my life except as a functional depressive.

During my quiet, introspective moments, I asked God many of life's bigger questions without receiving what I considered to be any definitive answers. I prayed for relief—some kind of sign that would validate that there was more to my life than merely jumping through everyone else's hoops. I didn't feel any deep sense of belonging with the significant people in my life, nor could I see any logical arrangement for how the pieces of the universe functioned together. Life appeared to be haphazard and arbitrary. I felt very alone with my struggle. I responded to my existential crisis by staying busy with my overloaded schedule, continuing to wear my social mask, and, to the greatest extent possible, preventing my despair from leaking out in unintended ways.

I spent most of my Saturdays at the barn. My mother spent her Saturdays at the barn as well, instructing beginning level riding students. For six years, without exception, I had ridden in the front seat en route to the barn. During the past six months, there were two other novice students accompanying us to the stable. I did not consider either of these girls to be friends of mine, merely passengers in our car who lived in close proximity to our home.

One spring day, I had been relegated to the backseat of the car. The week prior, Jane, one of the younger upstart girls, had insisted on usurping my designated place in the front, and my mother had promised that she could have the role of copilot in the cockpit on the successive Saturday. I took a seat behind my mother, and Veronica sat next to me behind the front passenger seat as we waited for Jane to arrive. After waiting a reasonable amount of time, Jane never appeared. This behavior was highly unusual. Jane had consistently and reliably accompanied us to the stable. Due to her absence, I promptly campaigned to resume my rightful place up front. My mother was adamant that I remain where I was, as we were now running late.

It was quite unusual for me to debate with my mother over anything, as I had learned that doing so never worked in my favor. For some inexplicable reason, I insisted that I be allowed to change seats, arguing that doing so would only take a minute. Looking back, I see that my need to sit up front was clearly a feeble way of trying to exercise control in a universe that felt indiscriminate to me. My mother became quite perturbed with my behavior, and I instantly recognized that I would be on thin ice if I took my argument further. Suddenly, I was also brought up short by a forceful and resolute voice in my mind that ordered me to stay put: *You will remain exactly where you are. Do you understand? You are not to move from this seat.*

This voice sounded exactly like my own—and yet it held my attention with a powerful, commanding quality that seemed to be coming at the behest of a source outside myself. Without any effort at all, my irritation immediately waned and I quickly acquiesced to the voice. It seemed crucial that I immediately take note and comply with the direction I had been given. At the same time, surprisingly, there was no struggle involved in doing so. My mind felt peaceful. In the next moment, my mother backed out of the driveway, and off we went.

I had traveled this two-lane country road hundreds of times. However, on this atypical day, I was abruptly jolted out of my complacency when I heard my mother utter, in a panicked voice, "Oh my God! I have to . . ." As the car began to skid to the left, my sensory system was bombarded with an insufferable screeching sound as the tires fought to grip the pavement. It felt as though time slowed down and sped up simultaneously. Adrenaline flooded my body as I braced myself, anticipating the upcoming impact. Our sturdy eight-cylinder Buick LeSabre collided with a black Cadillac, commandeered by a babysitter who was shuttling her four young charges home. This young girl had barreled through the stop sign, unwittingly thrusting her vehicle into our path. Glass shattered everywhere, sending tiny shards into my face. The garage door opener that had been attached to the driver's side visor flew like a missile, pummeling my forehead. I tried to manage my shock as I processed what I was observing. The demolished front passenger door had collapsed like a deflated accordion. It now rested against my mother's shoulder, crushing her purse in the process. Our car was completely totaled. It would eventually be hauled to a scrap yard.

I managed to step through my side door without any significant injuries. Veronica also managed to scoot out my side door, finding herself with just a few embedded glass shards as well. Amazingly, no one from either car was seriously harmed. Plus, two lives were unequivocally spared—Jane's and mine. There is no question that anyone riding in that passenger seat would have been killed on impact. I asked myself, what forces had conspired to ensure that Jane's date in the front seat was thwarted? Furthermore, what deliberate forces had ensured my survival? What exact set of second-by-second interchanges had to occur to have the exact point of impact result in the preservation of eight promising lives? What was I meant to understand as a consequence of this experience?

The skies never opened up to allow a heavenly host of angels to sing, nor did my depression spontaneously vanish. Life isn't necessarily that simple. I still had to solve my ongoing karmic lessons. I still ruminated on my cosmic musings. In 1971, I felt bereft because I was unable to clearly discern God's answers in the time frame my ego demanded.

Despite that circumstance, my prayers indeed were eventually answered. My angels did in fact intervene to keep me here. On that day, a sacred seed was planted in rich soil. I tentatively began to accept that my life was in fact significant—that all lives are miraculous and that each of us is here to embody a higher purpose. I slowly began to consider that my life's fabric consisted of a magnificently orchestrated divine plan that was greater than my perpetual adolescent strivings.

All of my experiences during my youth, including this so-called "spring accident," stood me in good stead for my future life path. Each of my challenges and gifts created the ideal spiritual soup that shaped and strengthened me to ultimately serve. Via my "accident," I discovered that life was miraculous on multitudinous levels. I began to realize that everything was indeed working together, all the time, for our greatest good. This principle is constantly operating, even though we may not necessarily possess the foresight or insight to grasp our divinely orchestrated action plans. As spiritual beings having a human experience, we hold the potential to embrace a higher perspective grounded in love, knowing that the Divine communicates and miracles abound each and every day.

❧ 18 ❧

A Father's Message

Vicki Higgins

After having a corporate, success-driven focus and shifting to a more spiritual, purposeful life, I connected with my inner guidance and began creating success from the inside. Spiritual growth became a priority.

One day I lay down to begin a guided meditation. I turned on the meditation recording and started doing breath work. While I breathed, I actually felt energy moving around me. It was almost like a little cat had jumped on the bed and was pushing on the blanket near my legs, trying to get my attention.

Hey, come play. Hey, come play, the energy seemed to say.

I've had some wild experiences, but this was something new altogether. There was something energetic pushing on my leg. I sat up and looked around. My cat was over in her cat tree, sound asleep, so it wasn't her nudging me.

"Huh, that's really interesting," I said to myself.

I didn't see anything, so I lay back down and continued my meditation.

The feeling of this energy pushing on my leg got stronger and stronger. I finally did a cleansing breath and said a little prayer: "If there is any energy in my room that isn't supposed to be here or that isn't for my highest good, then please let it leave. If this is for my highest good, or if this is an energy that really needs to communicate with me, then you're welcome to stay. I just don't know how to communicate with you."

When the energy feeling didn't leave, I stopped the meditation and decided to contact my sister. She has had a much longer path of spiritual awareness and a more focused ability to communicate with Spirit than I do. With my sister on speakerphone, I remembered hearing about a way to communicate with Spirit using a pendulum, which I just so happened to have left over from a spiritual class that I had taken some time before.

Dangling the pendulum before me, together we said, "Okay, spirit, you clearly can move energy. You can reach out and touch me and I can feel you. Maybe you can move this pendulum. Let's practice that now. Show us a yes."

It took a minute, but finally the pendulum started swinging left to right, left to right.

We then said, "Okay, if that's a yes, then show us a no."

The pendulum stopped and then began to move vertically, forward and backward, forward and backward.

"Okay," we surmised, "if horizontal is a yes and vertical is a no, then we can communicate with you."

Since my sister has more experience with these types of communications, she asked the next questions on our behalf.

"Have you been on earth?"

The pendulum moved horizontally to indicate yes.

"Have you passed away?"

Horizontal movement: yes.

"Have you been to the light?"

Again, yes.

"Now, you are here trying to get Vicki's attention, so there must be a reason for that?"

Yes.

"Do you know Vicki?"

Yes.

"Is this a message for her?"

Vertical movement: no.

"Is this a message for someone she knows?"

Yes.

As this communication continued, my sister tuned in to Spirit, and words began to come to her. She started to put things together, and finally asked me, "Did you have a fitness trainer that passed away? He knows you."

"Oh my gosh, yeah," I said.

She asked, "Is his name David or *Dahv-eed* or something?"

"Yeah. Oh my gosh, that's David. He was so impactful in my life a few years ago when I was working in Los Angeles."

While I was still in my corporate life, I was diagnosed with lupus, and additionally my job was causing an undue amount of stress. I struggled with the realization that I had a terminal illness and floundered to find a way to cope.

David was one of only four people in the world that I told. His attitude was always helpful, encouraging, and positive. He helped me figure out fitness and nutrition plans, but more than that, he helped me learn how to control my mind-set. He showed me new meditations, and he taught me that my mind can control my health.

He and I started working on meditations and the power of thought to change my health from the inside out. A couple weeks later, the doctors redid some tests and learned that lupus was a misdiagnosis. I was then categorized as having chronic fatigue syndrome. David even helped me to work through that and to bring physical and spiritual wellness into my life. I recovered fully and have amazing vitality now, thanks to this beautiful experience.

I always told David, "Gosh, you were like an angel to me. You really helped me hold it together through a really difficult and emotional time."

When I left my corporate job, moved, and transitioned to a more spiritual way of being, I unfortunately lost touch with him. Later, I heard that he had passed in a motorcycle accident. I was devastated, because I felt like I'd never thanked him properly for playing such an integral role in my life.

To hear that David was here, with me in my room, communicating through my sister, I knew instinctively that there was something important he needed to say. As my sister continued to ask questions, she received the color blue through her communication and asked, "What is blue?"

She received a mental picture of David's wife at an event, wearing blue—though she couldn't make out if it was a scarf, a skirt, or something else. He wanted us to know that he had been with her at that moment, when she wore blue.

David also conveyed to us that his second youngest child, Ann, was having a hard time with him being physically gone. He wanted us to deliver a message to his wife for Ann, so that Ann would know her father was still with her energetically, even though he was no longer in a physical body. He wanted them both to know that energy doesn't die, especially love. Love is energy and love is forever.

He also asked that we convey to Ann that it was okay for her to speak to her dad and to share and play and just continue to have a relationship with him. He asked us to tell all the children that he was with them and to tell his wife that he was with her and helping her on her path.

I wrote everything down and promised to get in touch with his wife to pass the message on.

This isn't my line of work. I am a speaker, an author, and a consultant; I'm not a psychic. I'd been working on my own spiritual growth, but to have this happen was really a beautiful and unique experience—and I was a little concerned about what David's wife might say when I contacted her. I'd only met her a handful of times, one being at David's funeral, so I thought she might dismiss me as some kind of crazy. But I'd promised David I would deliver his messages, so I contacted his wife through a Facebook message to set up a time to meet.

When that day came, I told Judy everything I had experienced, from the pushing energy to the messages David delivered through my sister, watching her for any negative reaction.

I then asked, "Were you at an event recently? What color were you wearing?"

She said, "Oh, yeah. I was at a concert, and I had a blue scarf."

She happened to have a photograph of her at the concert on her phone, and this bright white energy was all around her head and resting on her shoulders. It looked like arms around her. The photograph was stunning.

We both exclaimed, "Oh my gosh!" "That's totally David! That's so crazy."

I asked after the kids, since David had mentioned Ann's difficulties. Judy confirmed that Ann was taking her father's death particularly hard.

I told Judy that I was sorry to hear that, but I had a message for the kids—Ann particularly. "He wanted you to tell the kids, especially Ann, that it's okay to talk with him," I said. "He said it's okay for her to miss him. It's okay for her to play with him. It's okay for her to be joyful that he's around her and that he's helping her on her path."

Tears began to flow as Judy and I discussed David's life and his messages for his family from beyond. A deep connection of gratitude formed between us, and through us, with Spirit—and David, who I'm sure was watching our conversation with thankfulness and love. This whole experience was a confirmation to me that even though somebody passes, his or her energy is still available to us. Physical death doesn't mean our loved ones are gone forever. It just means they're in a different form. They're here with us energetically to help us on our path, to bring us love and guidance, and to bring us those inspired thoughts and messages.

Their love is eternal; we only need to open ourselves to the opportunity to continue our relationships in a new form.

The Mirror with a Message

Laurel Geise, DMin

During the time when Bob and I went from being coworkers to being partners in love and life, he would write me secret love messages on Post-It notes and hide them in my desk. He must have known it would thrill me in the midst of a busy workday to reach for a Post-It and unexpectedly see his distinctive rendition of a heart, with the words "I love you" written above it. Nothing brought on the butterflies like finding one of these love notes, or smelling his cologne—Obsession, by Calvin Klein—and knowing it meant he was nearby.

It didn't take long to figure out Bob was the love of my life. We soon found ourselves giggling in the middle of the night as we made plans to elope in Las Vegas. We decided Valentine's Day would be the perfect date and set about relishing every moment of our engagement. That Fourth of July weekend we had tickets to see Bob's favorite band, The Eagles. As we got dressed for the preconcert tailgate party, Bob told me he didn't feel well. I gave him an aspirin and suggested he lie down for a bit, hoping it would pass and he'd be able to enjoy the show.

But Bob's unwell feeling didn't pass. When he stepped out of the bedroom holding his chest, I was immediately seized by the terror of the situation—Bob was having a heart attack! I got him into the car and raced him to the hospital where he disappeared with doctors for several agonizing hours. At last, a doctor emerged to tell me Bob had survived. Lying in his hospital room with him that night, I watched the fireworks through the window, awash with gratitude. Silent tears streaming down my face, I listened to his breathing and pledged to cherish every moment we would spend together for the rest of our lives.

The next morning, when the doctor made his rounds, he told us he had good news and bad news. The good news was that Bob had survived the heart attack with minimal heart damage. The bad news was they had found a large tumor in his right lung that was most likely cancer. Further tests proved the tumor was malignant. The doctors believed Bob had six months to live.

During the grueling months that followed, though we got Bob every treatment available, the cancer continued to spread. Determined not to let Bob's condition interfere with our dream of getting married in Las Vegas, I started packing for the trip. Valentine's Day was fast approaching, and we knew it was now or never.

The day before our scheduled flight, Bob relapsed. We had no choice but to admit him into the hospital—but this time, he never left. We spent those final days together pledging our eternal love. We cried, laughed, and held each other as if we would never have to let go.

He was wrapped tightly in my arms on the morning he took his final breath. I'll never forget the silence that followed that breath. I began shaking uncontrollably, emotions stirring within me that I didn't even recognize as my own. I yelled at God. I was utterly consumed with grief, painfully alone.

I had a funeral to plan, and Bob had given me instructions. He wanted his funeral to be a celebration of his life, and he'd made me promise that I would play specific songs by The Eagles during the memorial service. I designed the service exactly as he had envisioned it, right down to the Hawaiian shirt he wore, his sunglasses in the breast pocket. The only way I failed him that day was in his request that I celebrate his life instead of mourning my loss. I was too deeply plunged into my own dark depression to even go through the motions of anything vaguely celebratory.

I was indescribably lonely. I longed for him. I especially missed lying with him on our couch in the living room, where he would hold me in his arms and I would soak up his comfort. Then it happened. Late one evening in the middle of the night, I tossed sleeplessly on that couch, thinking of him. Missing him. And then . . . Bob was there. I felt the solidness of his arms around me as he pulled me close to him. Every cell of my body was flooded with his love. My bones shook as I melted into his beautiful energy. Though the moment was fleeting, it was indescribably intimate, and I felt as though it lasted an eternity.

The experience rattled me to my core. I didn't know exactly what had happened; I just knew that I felt intensely, unconditionally loved and connected to Bob.

That hug from beyond this world radically shifted my beliefs about life after death. Maybe there was something to this afterlife thing I had heard about, and maybe Bob was still with me. Little did I know at the time of this first miracle that my curriculum on the true energetic nature of love had only just begun.

During the second year of my depression, I decided to reset my engagement ring. I couldn't ever bear to take it off after Bob died, and when strangers saw an engagement ring on my finger they'd naturally ask questions about my fiancé. My explanation of his death would quickly bring these conversations to abrupt, awkward ends, and I had hoped that having the stone reset might help me avoid these uncomfortable interactions. I even dared to hope it might help dissolve the cloud of sadness that followed me wherever I went.

Late one afternoon I stopped by the jewelry store to arrange for the new setting. I was the only customer in the shop so I was greeted immediately by the salesclerk. I began explaining the kind of setting I was looking for, showing her the ring Bob had given me. I abruptly stopped speaking when a strong scent filled the room. The clerk's facial expression made it clear she had noticed it too. She said, "Do you smell men's cologne?" We both glanced around the store, confused, as we were obviously the only ones in the building.

Then I recognized the scent: Calvin Klein's Obsession. My laughter bubbled up as I felt Bob's love surround me. He was there. He liked my idea for the ring. Through tears I tried to explain to the bewildered jewelry clerk what was happening, but she just looked at me as though I had two heads. Her astonishment made me laugh even harder. It was the second miracle teaching me that love exists beyond death.

Two more years passed and the whole world was making plans to celebrate the beginning of a new millennium. I was invited to spend New Year's Eve with Dr. Deepak Chopra and my fellow meditation instructors in Palm Springs, California. Deepak had taught me how to meditate and certified me as an instructor. My daily practice of meditation had helped me with my physical, emotional, and spiritual healing, and I knew I'd want to be surrounded by these friends as the clock ticked the start of the year 2000.

When I arrived in the desert, I immediately began to experience an overwhelming sense of loneliness. Feeling conspicuously out of place, I watched couple after couple check into the hotel. Everyone looked so happy, so excited, so filled with anticipation. Maybe I wasn't ready for celebrations. Maybe this whole thing had been a mistake. I opened the door to my beautiful hotel room and tried to focus on the amazing evening ahead, surrounded by loving friends.

But memories of my life with Bob bubbled up from deep within me. Memories of our laughter and incredible connection flooded my heart as tears flooded my eyes. I imagined what it would be like to share this special evening with him. He had loved to dance and was always the life of the party.

I told him I loved him, as I often did.

Eventually, I was able to take a deep breath and stop crying. I had made the trip across the country from Florida to California for this party. I was not going to stay in my hotel room, locked in the past, while everyone downstairs laid out a welcome mat for the future. Something told me a good, long shower was the key to pulling myself together.

I started the shower, making the water as hot as it would go. Standing in the steaming stream, I gave myself a much-needed motivating pep talk. I stood for a long time under the hot flow, praying for it to rinse away enough of my sadness to let me get through the night. Finally, I turned off the water and pulled back the shower curtain. Still standing in the shower, facing the bathroom mirror, I felt chills go through my body. Something unusual had caught my eye through the clouds of steam. A message was written on the mirror.

The steam slowly dissipated until I could clearly make out what was etched into the condensed water droplets. The words, "I love you," above a heart. There was no mistaking the handwriting or the distinctive shape of Bob's hand-drawn heart. I had seen this butterflies-inducing message on too many Post-It notes not to recognize it for exactly what it was, what it always had been—an expression of eternal love from the man I adored.

I stood paralyzed by a combination of awe, love, and magic that literally took my breath away. He had heard me profess my love for him, and he wanted me to know that he loved me too. Our love *was* eternal. I thought to myself, *No one will ever believe this.* And in the same moment, I knew it didn't matter.

My heart was beating so hard it shook my whole body. I said a prayer of gratitude as the tears flowed. Standing in the timeless moment of that third miracle, I was flooded with an energy of love so powerful I thought I would collapse. I knew each miracle had been architected to show me that our soul mates never leave us. They simply accompany us through time, always connected to us. Bob was with me.

I got dressed, went to the party, and made a champagne toast to our love. I embraced the new millennium, knowing deep in my heart that I had a lifetime of miracles ahead of me.

⌒ 20 ⌒

The Golden Eiffel Tower

Christie Melonson, PhD

Ever since I was a child, I remember having the most vivid and colorful dreams. They were more action-packed than movies, and sometimes they even showed me what was going to happen in the future. Throughout the years my dreams have become even more vibrant, intense, and prophetic. Sometimes they are so spot-on that loved ones call me to ask if I have been dreaming about them lately. They want to know if they will get a new job, have a baby, or if their health will improve.

Once I had a dream about an Apache medicine man who was planning to move away from his home. In the dream, I saw him speaking to another man, and I could recall the exact words of their conversation. It didn't mean anything to me—not until I actually met the man in my dreams. When I told him the dream I had had about him, he was shocked and impressed, because all that I had dreamed had actually happened! He told me that I was given the gift of dreams to help guide and direct others.

Soon after that encounter I began to dream of my Native American ancestors who told me I was meant to be the "voice of the tribe." I dreamt of a woman who called herself Pé. She was beautiful and earthly and wore old clothing that looked as though it was from the nineteenth century. I immediately felt drawn to her, and I was calm in her presence. When I woke, I called my mother and described this woman. My mom told me that I was describing my great-great-grandmother, Pélage, a Native American woman from Louisiana. Knowing that my great-great grandmother was guiding me, I made a conscious decision to be open-minded about the power and significance of my dreams.

As I learned to listen to my dreams, they became more and more helpful over the years. For example, I often recall dreaming about pop quizzes in college before they happened and knowing when my car would break down or when my boss would be in a bad mood. I'm a practical person, so I learned to listen to my dreams and the dreams of others. I have often encouraged others to pay close attention to their dreams and the messages within them—especially messages from loved ones.

In the recent past, my dreams have gone from being helpful to healing and absolutely life changing. While I was working on my dissertation, I began to have dreams about my father's parents, who are deceased. They would come to visit in my dreams to tell me that my dad was having health problems. That last summer, his parents spoke to me in a dream that was so powerful it woke me up, as though I was being hit with a heavy shock.

Shortly after, my dad had his first heart attack.

When my dad's heart stopped, mine broke at the same time. I recall sitting in the hospital and praying nonstop. During this time he, too, saw his parents in his dreams. I thought he would be swayed to follow them to the other side—and I wasn't ready to lose my dad yet. I talked to my grandparents in my dreams and told them they couldn't take him anywhere! I don't know whether they listened to me, or if he simply chose not to transition yet, but thankfully my dad is still here with me today.

I put my dissertation on hold while I worked to help my dad regain his health. My dissertation chair, Sister Dot, told me to take my time and that she would be waiting when I returned.

It was at this time that I also began having interesting dreams about Sister Dot. She was a woman I greatly admired, a superintelligent nun/psychologist with a very powerful presence. In the dreams, she was telling me that it was time for me to deliver and that I needed to get on the birthing table. I wasn't pregnant in real life or in the dreams, and I recall looking at my not so round belly wondering what she was talking about.

Once dad had recovered from his heart attack, I returned to school to finish my doctoral studies. I was relieved and ready to meet with Sister Dot to finalize the plans for my dissertation. But when we had made plans to discuss my work, she uncharacteristically canceled our meeting. That same night, I dreamed of Sister Dot again—this time, though, I dreamed that she grabbed me by the hand and told me it was time to defend my dissertation. I told her I wasn't ready and that I was scared, but she encouraged me and congratulated me afterward, telling me how easy it was. I was relieved by her reassurances and felt ready to get down to work.

The next morning, though, my school announced that Sister Dot had had two strokes and was placed in hospice. I was crushed, especially because she had been my mentor and friend from the beginning of my studies.

She was the person who convinced me that I was smart enough and good enough to become a doctor at a time when I seriously doubted my academic abilities.

I felt it when Sister Dot passed away. I knew the exact moment she transitioned, because I dreamed of a crucifix and then saw her face along with a bright flash of white light. The next day, the school announced her passing. I remember feeling numb and heavy with sadness. My mentor was gone. Who was I to look up to? I felt lost, like there was a piece of me missing. I didn't know who would ever be able to fill the hole in my heart that Sister Dot's death had created, and I was despondent that I would never hear her wise council again. I begged her for a sign that she was still with me, that she was still supporting and rooting for me.

Just a few days later, as I lay in bed, I saw her again. She looked much younger than she had in all the time I had known her, and she was smiling brightly. She said: *You know, we can see everything you are doing from up here!* She laughed and hugged me and kissed me on the cheek. I watched her introduce herself to my grandmother and others I knew, both alive and deceased, in a big meeting room. I felt a strong sense of warmth and woke up with a jolt of energy that morning. I knew she was still around and was cheering for me from heaven. It made all the difference in the world to have that dream. She renewed my hope for successfully finishing my studies. Just as she'd said in previous dreams, it was time to birth my dissertation—and she would be right there with me, all along.

When I first started to experience these dreams, I didn't know how to feel about their accuracy. As I opened myself to this experience and learned to accept my gift, as the Apache medicine man called it, I found that these dreams were sent to me not to be frightening, but simply to be guidance toward my greatest good. These days, I fall asleep knowing I am never alone, especially in the face of challenges, and I am surrounded by once earth-bound angels who support me in my life and communicate through my dreams.

I now believe more than ever that life continues after death, and that our loved ones still look out for us from beyond the grave. My dreams have given me direction in life, offered explanations for life events, and have shown me that I am loved, especially when I felt very alone. I share my dream stories with you to inspire you to look deeply into the significance of your own. Through my dreams I have seen a glimpse of how the Divine can be intertwined with the commonplace. Even in moments when we feel we are drifting alone through life, our dreams can show us that we are still surrounded by boundless and limitless love, and that we are being guided by forces unseen. In the midst of life challenges, the Divine and our loved ones send us messages to give us hope and to encourage us to persevere, frequently through dreams. Sleep well, and embrace the blessings brought forth during your slumber!

My Mother's Gift

Kim Dayoc

Mom furrowed her brows, pointed her finger at me, and gave me her last words. "You little shit. I wish I would have never had you!" Her finger, pointed directly at my face, withdrew, and she sneered at me in anger. My mother was lying on a hospital gurney waiting to be rolled into another room for another test. She was dying of cancer; it had spread all over her body into every major organ, including her brain.

"Wow, Mom," was all I could utter. I stood there staring at her, astonished. "There went my Movie of the Week moment!" I added, unsure what else I could say to such vitriol. I knew this was the last time I would see her and had asked her if there was anything she wanted to tell me. *The scene I had imagined is that my mother would apologize for abandoning me and tell me she loved me. I cry, mom cries, the audience cries, scene fades to black. However, this was not a Lifetime movie.* Neither one of us cried. We just stared at one another. As the nurse pushed her down the hall, I stood in the same spot, taking in that last moment with my mother. I was not surprised she chose to attack me. It was her pattern for all of my life.

Our family imploded when my parents divorced. I was nine years old. My father had an affair and my mother refused to forgive him. When he left, he married his mistress, and my mother started her descent into reclusive darkness. She was emotionally unstable and violent. Her health deteriorated along with her mind due to multiple strokes. Her face, already aging into a permanent frown, was distorted. I was in the sixth grade when my brother died on his sixteenth birthday. My mother lost herself, and she completely stopped caring for me.

One morning before school, I went into her bedroom, crying. She was in her usual spot: the right side of her bed, lying on her side, covers over her head. I told her I had nothing to wear. She pointed to her closet and told me to pick something from there. A young, seventh-grade girl doesn't look normal wearing her grown mother's clothes. I found a skirt I hoped would work and then I went to my closet and sat down. I looked up and began sobbing as I looked at all the empty hangers. I literally had no clothes.

We received food stamps, but the free school lunch was the biggest meal of my day. I learned to do my own laundry; I cleaned the house and mowed the yard. I took care of what I could, believing that if I could make things better, my mother would snap out of her depression and love me again.

When I was fourteen, Mom kicked me out of her house. It was a tumultuous time, and eventually I came back for a few months but left for fear that she was going to hurt me while I slept.

And then it happened. One Sunday morning while I was napping, I opened my eyes to see her standing over me, attempting to burn me in my sleep. I left the house immediately to stay with friends, and while I was gone, she moved to Pennsylvania without a forwarding address.

I'd always heard the old joke of how parents should move away once their kids hit their teen years and come back once they are adults—but no one ever did that, right? My mother, apparently, did not think it was a joke. I was alone in my hometown of San Antonio, and friends opened their homes. I survived. I tend to think I was blessed so many families took me in and that "the village" saw me through!

I grew and thrived and eventually started a family of my own. I thought of my mother, but I never tried to make contact. I was done with her, as she was sure to be done with me. Then one day I received a call from my sister Gail. It was a big surprise, as my family was in Germany for my husband's job in the army. One short phone call could cost a hundred dollars, so our friends and family in the States didn't call unless it was an emergency. Gail told me my mother was dying and she had asked to see my two young daughters. She had only seen my eldest a few times and had never met the younger one. I was perplexed she asked to see the girls, as she had held no interest in my family, or me, ever.

I had three options laid out before me: go and see her while she was alive, go for the funeral, or do not go at all. It was a tough debate, but in the end I opted to see her while she was alive.

My father walked into her hospital room first. We gave him a moment with her, and when we entered, he was sobbing. She just laid there, staring at him. My mother had been a beautiful bride, but life had ravaged her and left a twisted shell. Her struggles and illnesses destroyed her outer beauty. Her face was distorted from multiple strokes, her teeth were gone, and she struggled with her speech. My daughters came up behind their grandfather, and my mother sat up to see them. "Oh, h-h-how n-nice," she stammered. That was it; grandmother bonding was over.

I sat down next to her and my father. His face red from emotion, he looked over at me and said, "She looks like you, Jane. She has your hair."

"Beautiful," my mother commented, her voice strangely clear.

I was overcome by emotion at this exchange, so I ran out of the room. My tears came from such a deep part of my soul, they almost hurt. My mother and father had *never* talked about me like that before. After I pulled myself together, I went back in the room. Eventually, we arranged for hospice care, much against my mother's wishes to "never end up in a nursing home." We thought she would pass any day, but the days stretched into weeks, and it soon became impossible for us to remain in the States. We had to return to Germany.

Three weeks after we got home, the Red Cross contacted my husband to tell him that my mother had passed—but I didn't learn this news for another two and a half days. While sitting on his chair, eating a bowl of cereal, he remembered. "Kim," he said, talking with his mouth full of Cheerios, "I forgot to tell you, your mother didn't make it." He took another big bite of cereal.

"Didn't *make* it? What are you saying?" I said.

"She's dead."

"Oh."

I got up and left for our room, asking him to watch the girls. I needed some time alone. I had had no idea that her passing would hurt so much. My husband stopped me and said, "You and your mother didn't like each other; why are you acting like this?"

I didn't have an answer, as I had asked myself that same question. I ached, I mourned, I rolled up in a ball and wished for my mommy. I guess I had wished that all of my life, and with her alive there was hope that one day she would show up. I was mourning the loss of my hope. I spent two nights in our room crying and confused as to why her death had the impact it was having.

The second night of mourning was the same as the first. I was broken. I kept hearing her last words to me, calling me a little shit when all I wanted was reconciliation. That night, while I lay sleeping, I suddenly heard someone tell me to wake up. I looked up, and there she was. She was standing beside my bed, glowing. I could not see past her because she was surrounded by light. I noticed her hair. It appeared so soft, and I could see every separate strand. Her face was beautiful and flawless. From pictures i had seen, I would say she was in her late twenties, youthful and restored. She was wearing a blue dress. I sat up in bed and touched her face. She was so kind, so full of love.

I came to tell you I am sorry and that I love you now the way I should have always loved you. I am perfect now; my love is perfect. I will be with you always, she said. Then she held me.

I cried again, though this time it was not so painful, but felt healing instead.

I woke sitting up in bed. My mother was gone, and I immediately woke up my husband. "She was here!" I cried. "She was here!" I told him everything. "I think she knew she really hurt me with her last words, and God let her come back to tell me she was sorry!"

My husband told me I was dreaming, rolled back over, and continued to sleep. In the morning I woke up feeling excited and happy. I then began to question the vision. It seemed real, but my husband didn't believe me, and he didn't see anything, either. I doubted what I had seen.

My husband came home at noon with the day's mail. I received a letter from my father's wife. She had sent a page torn out of a popular Christian magazine. She highlighted several things on the page. First, she highlighted the date—July 8th, my birthday. Second, she had highlighted the title, which was about relationships. There were a couple sentences under the yellow glow: "If a person dies in Christ and the relationship was bad, remember, with Christ all things become perfect. The relationship is perfected."

Almost word for word, the article echoed what my mother had told me in my vision. The article continued with a message to forgive, and I knew it was a sign that I needed to unpack my emotional baggage. I was given a gift. She had been perfected, and I needed to forgive her earthly mistakes. Now I know that she is with Christ, and as I unpacked my "Mother didn't love me" bags, I knew she was with me, as well, just as she is with Christ: perfected. She is beautiful, radiant, and full of light and love. Now she is Mommy, the mommy I always loved, adored, and needed, and despite her abandonment of me in the physical world, I know that now, in the spiritual, she will always be with me.

❧ 22 ❧

The Gift

Thea Alexander

I was delivering a eulogy, speaking through the tears welling up from deep within that streamed from my eyes. My chest felt tight with anguish as I tried to relay what a loving man my father was, how different our lives would be without him, and how deeply he would be missed.

I woke with a start.

I had been awoken from a dream about giving my father's eulogy only to be told of his actual passing.

In the early morning hours, slipping silently from physical presence, my father graduated his earthly existence. Following a ten-year relationship with cancer, all he was meant to experience was accomplished. Lives touched, lessons acquired, moments created and shared.

On the day of my father's funeral, we were honored to experience him in spirit. Traveling through country back roads, the procession slowly made its way to the small cemetery located on the edge of town. Approaching the site, we noticed a prominent tree across the road from the cemetery. A humongous maple, gnarled, weathered, and dead, stood like a guard at the cemetery's entrance.

An American bald eagle sat perched like a sentinel in its boughs. The eagle was my father's favorite bird, and the maple his favorite tree. Undoubtedly, Dad was there with us as we gathered in his honor to place his human form in its final resting place.

When spring came, I visited my father's farm, where he had lived for nearly twenty years. Out in the yard stood a giant mountain ash, another tree significant to my father, as he had spent many years pampering that poor old tree in an effort to coax one season of red-orange berries out of it, its hallmark feature. It had never worked—except after his death. This season, ample leaves covered its aging branches, more so than in the past decade, and midway through summer it developed berries in clumps so heavy the lower branches drooped to kiss the earth. After this spectacular and spontaneous bloom, the tree died a few weeks later and had to be removed. This was just the first of many signs from my father.

In the days and weeks following his death, I began to experience life far beyond the human experience. Feeling as though I was coming home to myself, I accepted unquestionably that it all lay dormant within me and was now awakening. My budding awareness of the life force within, my soul, felt familiar and comfortable.

A mere two months after his passing, I was resting on my bed, relaxed in the space between sleep and wakefulness. I felt someone lay beside me, yet no one was there. I wasn't frightened, but I knew that I also was not alone.

While I physically lay in bed, my soul began a journey that I vividly remember. In a vision, my brother and I traveled a long and lonely highway in the Canadian wilderness of Ontario, struggling to reach a safe haven before nightfall.

With every turnoff and intersection came disappoint-ment as we were unable to find the refuge we sought. We decided to turn back instead of risking going farther in the dark. Defeated and bereft, we slowed then veered to the right, turning slightly onto a sloping road we would have otherwise missed. There before us was the cabin we had instinctively sought . . .

As we approached the cabin, three splashing foun-tains beckoned me to look in their direction. Doing so, I marveled that somehow it was now just shortly after sunrise. Turning back toward the cabin, I saw that it too had changed and now resembled a great log lodge.

We proceeded up the stairs, across the grand deck, and pushed open the heavy wooden door. I looked around this unfamiliar place, focusing now on a glass display case that held candy and tourist trinkets, with a cash register atop and a glass tray of peppermint can-dies. The figure behind the case came slowly into focus, and we were greeted by a familiar voice. My aunt, who had passed away twenty years ago, laughingly exclaimed, "Well, look what the cat dragged in!" Greeting us with a warm welcome, she boldly stated, "I know who you're here to see." Quickly turning on her heel, she led us across a large room with vaulted ceilings, great log beams, and a wall of windows that opened into the vast Canadian wilderness.

Busy surveying the room, taking it all in, I was too dis-tracted to notice where we were going. The space aglow from the now morning sun, people filled booths lining the edges of the room, and others sat at tables scattered throughout the space. An inaudible din of conversation in the background set the tone and energy of the room. We stopped suddenly, and my aunt moved aside. Sitting there at a small table was a petite and frail man in a familiar flannel shirt, donning an even more familiar cap.

My father stood to welcome us with a wide, toothy grin and a warmhearted hug, as he always had when he was still living. He exuded joy. It was literally radiating from him like a warm-toned glow. He motioned for us to sit.

He began by asking how the drive was, and we made small talk. As we conversed, the rest of the room (including my brother) faded into the background. Soon it was just Dad and me talking, laughing, reminiscing, and crying together there in that magical space. It felt so good to see him! I was giddy and unable to focus completely, at first. All I knew was how wonderful it felt to be near him once again, to hear his voice, and to have an opportunity to "catch up."

I remember thinking, *This can't be real—he's dead.* But it was very real. I couldn't make up the conversations we were having. Not in a million years. He carefully and thoughtfully attended to every detail, every question, every emotion raised within me as we reviewed our lives together. Attentively, compassionately, and lovingly he showed me our life circumstances from a very different perspective, one of unconditional love, absolute acceptance, and in a space completely void of judgment. Nothing was labeled or defined; it just was. I was able to appreciate every detail, from our perspectives and also from a very different place outside of human existence, a space that allowed each interaction to be a vital lesson for the energy within me, my soul.

As suddenly as it began, it was over. My brother reappeared as if from thin air. He stated it was time to leave, briefly detailing the long drive that lay ahead. Knowing he was right, Dad and I pushed our chairs back from the table and rose in unison, exchanging pleasantries of how nice it was to see each other again and how thankful we were for our time together.

I said, "I love you. There is so much I want to share with you. Do you really have to go?"

He responded, "I love you too, Boo," and spread his arms wide.

Stepping toward him, I melted into his embrace, suddenly aware that he was transparent. Rocking back on my heels, I stated, "Daddy, I don't understand. What's happening?"

My father replied, "You will have to hug me a little harder. I can't quite feel everything the same way from where I am now. Open your heart. Step in front of the fear." In that moment the entire day played out in my mind's eye, as I stood before him. A fast-forward version of the comings and goings, our telepathic conversations, the sunlight as it danced across the room, casting shadows as the end of day neared. I now realized that I saw everything through my father's image. He smiled and nodded, a knowing nod, acknowledging my new truth. He said, "There is no end. We continue beyond physical life. I am always with you."

Everything faded, and I became more aware of my surroundings as the veil between spirit and physical presence thinned. I smelled my father all around me and began to weep. I wept for the ache, deep within me, to have him here in the physical world. I wept for the ending of our time together in spirit. I wept too for the depth of his presence and the unconditional love I felt.

Surreal and profound.

Now, some ten years later, I remember the details as vividly as the day they occurred. Forever imprinted in my physical mind, this vision left an impression within my soul. I know, without a doubt, I am from that place and will return to unconditional love, a place beyond physical life, a place where my father's presence will be waiting for me.

✎ 23 ✎

Moving Beyond Fear

Jessica McKay

I was twenty-eight years old and working in the admissions office of a college in my hometown. I'm not sure it's possible to convey how much I hated the job or how out of place I felt. Every day was the same, every task was the same, and every morning, at the same time, my boss walked past our offices to make sure we were in our seats. I felt like I was suffocating. In my soul's longing for self-expression, I rebelled in my own small way, breaking the dress code one morning to wear red Converse sneakers. That was the best I could do to add some color to my life. And it was short-lived, as I was immediately called into my boss's office and reprimanded.

All the people I knew in my age group were either getting married, having children, or getting their master's degrees. I didn't have a plan for my life. I *couldn't* plan because I didn't know what I wanted, but I knew what I *didn't* want—to spend the rest of my life commuting to an office cubicle to do work I wasn't passionate about. I sensed that there was a different destiny for me, but I didn't know what it was. I only knew that I craved adventure and magic, and I gravitated toward spirituality.

My mother and father hated their jobs, too, and I thought that was simply what work was all about: doing something you hate in order to survive financially. And yet I clung to the hope that somehow there would be a different path for me.

At the time, I used solitary travel as a way to gain perspective about my life. I needed a vacation badly. But aside from major holidays, winter was "crunch time" at the office, and my colleagues and I weren't allowed vacations from December through April. In an act of desperation, I booked a one-week trip to London anyway. On the day of my departure, my dad called the office and told my boss I had the flu and wouldn't be in for a week.

Dad was a powerful ally, because he was able to relate to my feelings of being trapped. He couldn't stand his job as a cabdriver and wanted to see me enjoy my life as much as possible. Even when I was in kindergarten, he tried to rescue me with a few moments of freedom. He'd come and hang out with me while the other students napped. We'd sit outside on the stone steps, eating the apples and grapes he brought, and I'd be so grateful for the temporary escape from what I considered to be my prison. Even then, I hated being boxed in and he knew it.

So thanks to Dad, on New Year's Eve, I flew to London. I needed space to think about my life and what I wanted. I needed a different perspective, and more than anything, I needed evidence that I could become unstuck from my day-to-day reality and completely redesign my life. I said a frantic prayer as the plane sped down the runway: "Please, God, show me another way to live my life." I didn't want to return home without an answer and a new way forward.

When I arrived, London embraced me. Even though it was winter, it felt like a refuge from the cold drudgery of my life. I arrived at my hostel in the middle of the day, put my suitcase down, and fell asleep in my clothes. A few minutes before waking, I had a vivid dream. In the dream, a woman with auburn hair and shining eyes came to my room and shook me awake, saying that if I went to a bookstore, I would meet someone special. I awoke, and, still half asleep, stumbled down the lane. I had no idea where I was going, or even if anything was open late in the evening on New Year's Eve. I didn't stop to ask for directions; I just followed my feet. I walked three blocks, instinctively turned to my right, and there it was—a brightly lit Barnes & Noble that was open in spite of the holiday. I went directly to the New Age section, where I was always drawn in bookstores, and, looking up, I saw a man in an armchair reading a book.

The title of the book he was reading seemed to fly across the room. *Beyond Fear,* it said. The moment I saw that book, I knew it was the reason for my journey to the store. I don't know how I knew that; I just felt guided, as if I were a puppet whose strings were being operated by a higher consciousness. I read the subtitle as I grabbed the book from the shelf: *The Teachings of Don Miguel Ruiz on Freedom and Joy as recorded by Mary Carroll Nelson.*

Don Miguel Ruiz is the author of *The Four Agreements,* a book about Toltec wisdom that became a best seller after Ellen DeGeneres and Oprah recommended it in the late nineties. I had read *The Four Agreements* and appreciated it, but I had never seen *Beyond Fear* before. The title impacted me because fear was ruining my life. I was afraid of everything! I was afraid of change, I was afraid of close-ness in relationships, I was afraid to be myself.

As the book rested in my hands, I knew I needed to buy it. I spent the entire week in London reading the book from cover to cover. It was fascinating and told Miguel's story of the magical vision he had while visiting the sacred city of Teotihuacan, Mexico. In his vision, he saw that the ancient city was built as a university for spiritual seekers to come and learn the truth about life and about themselves. I felt something stir from deep within and decided to go there.

By the time I picked up this book, don Miguel Ruiz had gotten so famous as an author and teacher that he wasn't able to personally teach everyone who wanted to learn about Toltec wisdom. As a result, he had a list of teachers that he personally recommended who were taking their own groups on spiritual journeys to Mexico. One in particular, Allan Hardman, caught my attention. Allan is the creator of Joydancer.com, a website and a community of people all looking for their personal free-dom via the Toltec path as taught by don Miguel Ruiz. I made plans to contact Allan as soon as I got home.

I went back to my job feeling renewed. I did my ordinary work and sat in my cubicle wearing the proper work shoes, but inside, I was ecstatic. I had a plan and knew where to go for answers. As soon as the vacation ban was lifted at the office, I immediately booked a spot on Allan Hardman's next trip to Teotihuacan.

Teotihuacan is an ancient city of pyramids ninety minutes north of Mexico City. Our group walked from the hotel to the pyramid complex every day. We jour-neyed from structure to structure and plaza to plaza, doing personal ceremonies and rituals—letting go of fears, childhood trauma, and limiting beliefs with the support of the group. This is the journey that don Miguel Ruiz saw in his vision and describes in *Beyond Fear*.

My journey to Mexico forever changed the way I saw myself and the world. I found that most of my deeply held beliefs were false. I did *not* have to work at a job I hated to survive financially. I did *not* have to pretend to be what I thought people wanted so I could be accepted and loved. I learned that I could be vulnerable and people would still like me. I understood that my life situation was a reflection of my self-judgments, and now I was being introduced to just what I prayed for—"another way to live my life"—a way to live in love and self-acceptance.

Two months after my trip to Mexico, I quit my job and moved from New Jersey to California to work for Allan, assisting him with the business side of Joydancer. com. Moving to California felt like going home. The people I met were similar to me, with the same desire to go within, heal the stories that made them suffer, and create lives of joy. I found my soul family. I learned how to love myself and be happy. I began teaching with Allan and coleading his trips to Mexico. I developed an intense interest in emotional healing and signed up for hypnotherapy training. Studying hypnotherapy brought me into contact with my guardian angels and spirit guides for the first time—including the guide who had appeared in my dream.

A few years later, I was invited to narrate the official audio version of *Beyond Fear*. I went from being clueless and not knowing what I wanted to being a spiritual teacher and the voice that thousands of people hear when they listen to the audio version of the book. And it was all because my spirit guide came to visit me, all alone in a tiny hotel room on a holiday, thousands of miles away from anyone I knew, in an answer to my prayer. This one miracle opened the door to the rest of my life.

❧ 24 ❧

The Heart of an Intuitive Parent

Debra J. Snyder, PhD

At one time, intuition and energy didn't play a significant role in my life. Although I often sensed things, like the next song coming up on the radio or who was going to call later in the day, I gave the ability little consequence. I certainly didn't expect my newborn child would be my spiritual guide to unexplored corners of the universe, but Raegan's birth triggered an immediate, dramatic shift in my perspective on life.

A healthy pregnancy ended abruptly when my daughter was born with a rare brain malformation. My husband Mark and I felt as though our entire world turned on its side. Our thoughts and dreams came crashing down around us, replaced by a frightening, chaotic reality. We felt utterly alone and unprepared to handle what was before us. Little did we know at the time that a force beyond normal, physical reality would be there to lovingly embrace us.

Like most new parents, we were sleep deprived, with dark circles and relentless bed head. Mark and I took turns pacing the floor at 2:00 a.m., trying to calm our precious bundle and get a grip on life with special needs. Most evenings I fell asleep on the couch, sitting up with her lying on my chest. One late night, as Raegan and I sat quietly in the darkened living room trying to ease into sleep, I began to panic. This had occurred periodically before—a sensation that a forest was closing in around me, hiding the path ahead. This forest of fear grew increasingly dark and dense, my mind a flurry with a million disorganized thoughts. How would we get by? What would I do about my job? What if Raegan died? My heart raced and tears flowed down my face. I rose and paced the floor, my chest getting tight. I was ramping myself up into a panic attack, anxious thoughts dragging me into a deep chasm of despair. The room begin to pulse and swirl around me as I collapsed back onto the couch in a daze.

Through half-open eyes, I saw two figures move toward me. One of them took Raegan out of my arms, cradling her, whispering soft lullabies. The other sat beside me, stroking my face and hair. *Feel the light inside you. Let it guide you,* she said. *Your daughter is not afraid and feels confident in your care. You chose this. She chose this. We will be here to help you.*

These serene figures were hard to distinguish in the dark room. They weren't exactly people and seemed to change shape, color, and size right in front of me. The harder I tried to see them, the fainter they became. "Don't go!" I called as I startled awake. Raegan was sleeping tenderly on my chest, and no one else was in the room. Looking around, I felt deep recognition, as though I'd just visited with my great-grandmother had who had died when I was a child. "Nana," I cried aloud, "please come back!" Taking a deep breath, I placed Raegan into her crib and went to bed. Ten hours later, I awoke. We had both slept soundly for the first time since coming home from the hospital when Raegan was born.

I soon began to hear from others. One night, while asleep in our beds, I heard *Deb!*

"What?" I asked of Mark, who was lying beside me. There was no reply, as he was sound asleep.

Deb, now! the voice insisted. I abruptly sat up, trying to figure out what was going on and whether or not I was dreaming. My body tensed. "Raegan needs me," I whispered. I bounded from my bed and ran to her. My daughter's limp arm was dangling from her crib. She was pinned between the rails, a blanket covering her face, her body unmoving.

"Oh my God!" I cried as I grabbed her, removing her arm from the slatted side and lifting her tenderly up to me. She was fine and still sleeping. "Thank you . . . thank you . . . thank you for watching over us," I cried, not sure who or what I was thanking. My ancestors or maybe angels? It didn't matter to me; I was just glad someone was there.

Even though her disability was severe, we settled into a comfortable groove. Raegan, at almost three years old, lay motionless a few feet away from me, connected to numerous monitors and machines in the largest hospital in our state. We had been there for weeks, recovering from surgery to place a gastric feeding tube, as she was increasingly having trouble swallowing liquids without choking. Her small body lay lifeless, her eyes closed, with only the sounds of the equipment penetrating the air.

Now, in this bleak moment, it seemed that everything that could go wrong did go wrong. The complications following the procedure were numerous: a twisted stomach, inaccurate medications, and uncontrollable seizures. Each issue seemed to be addressed as they arose, yet Raegan wasn't doing well and we didn't know why. Her radiant smile and joyful laugh had been absent for days now.

My pleas for more tests were met with condescending remarks about overreactive parents, and I was advised not to question the wisdom and experience of a talented surgeon. As my daughter lay dying, I said a prayer of surrender to God: "Dear Lord, you know best. Please take care of my girl. Ease her pain. Whatever you want, just please show me the way to help her." Head drooping and shoulders hunched in resignation, I sighed deeply and continued to quietly weep.

Sitting there in the dark, physically and emotionally exhausted, warm tears rolling down my face, the phrase *It's growing* popped into my mind. Startling awake from my vacant gaze at the floor, I asked aloud, "What's growing?" Her reply was immediate. *In my throat, Mommy.* I leaped from my position on the bench to my daughter's side and said to her in a gentle voice, "Are you trying to tell me something, Angelbaby?" A resounding *Yes* flooded my body. She remained sleeping with no physical indication that she was communicating with me. This time I knew it wasn't an angel or spirit guide trying to get my attention—Raegan herself was reaching out to me for help. I didn't know how she was doing it, yet at that moment I believed with all my heart it was truth she was conveying.

The surgical team was resistant to anything I said. When I explained my concerns came directly from my daughter herself, they literally rolled their eyes.

After weeks of heated debate, with our daughter getting worse each day, they finally ordered more testing. They found that a surgical stitch had been misplaced during her procedure, causing scar tissue to grow around it, blocking her esophagus and leaving her unable to swallow. Now it was apparent. This grave circumstance was not due to her disability or a preexisting condition. She was a victim of a surgical mistake and was calling out for help. My daughter, who had no ability to speak, miraculously found a way to communicate and save her own life!

Raegan had to have additional surgery to correct the problem. Our confidence shaken in the original surgical team, we transferred hospitals and began the task of recovery. Throughout the many months she was hospitalized, Raegan continued to teach me how to use our hearts to talk. This unusual form of communication seemed especially acute during times of crisis and when we were both sleeping. At that point, I decided I would no longer make any decision regarding her care without checking in via our heart connection. It seemed to me Raegan was operating from a higher place.

However, fear and doubt still crept into my mind, as I worried I had made the wrong decision to leave our home to connect with a different hospital staff and surgical team. We had not yet met our new doctors, and, arriving so late at night, I didn't have the chance to get my bearings. "Please, God . . . give me a sign I have made the right decision," I whispered.

The door opened suddenly, and a vibrant young nurse came in. "Good morning and welcome, Miss Raegan," she said in a cheerful tone. "I'm here to make sure you are settling in. How are you doing, Mom? Would you like to walk around a bit and grab a cup of coffee while I get to know Raegan?" she asked sweetly. I knew my girl was in good hands for the few moments it would take me to find some caffeine.

Still watching them over my shoulder, I walked out of the room and abruptly collided with a man in the hall. He was an older gentleman with the kindest eyes, immaculately dressed in a suit and tie. A bit startled, I watched him walk into the room next to ours and say good morning to the folks inside. My heart still pounding, I realized I had just about knocked down the doctor, world-famous for his achievements in child development, T. Berry Brazelton.

Although Dr. Brazelton would not be involved in Raegan's care, I knew his presence was God giving me the sign I had asked for. Of all the doctors I could have plowed into and never recognized, *he* was put in my path. A chance encounter in the hall showed me we were in the company of some of the best specialists in the world; my daughter would be well cared for.

The miraculous signs have continued every day of our life, some subtle and others grand. Raegan is now sixteen years old and has been an amazing ambassador for the unlimited power of love and energy communication, for the miracles in every moment. It has brought me beyond the life of a casual intuitive to embracing intuition and energy as my life's purpose. Although our journey has not been an easy one, I am comforted in knowing no matter what comes our way the miracles of the universe will support my beautiful daughter and her intuitive parent.

⤜ 25 ⤛

Miraculous Cracks

Karen James

My heart has been cracked open more times than I can count. After surviving an abusive, alcoholic father, a teen pregnancy, and my father's suicide, I believed I had weathered the greatest storms life could possibly brew up for me. I was wrong. I considered myself an expert at patching my heart's cracks, but nothing—I mean nothing—could have prepared me for the crack that was yet to come.

Prior to the event that brought me to my knees, I'd spent many years finally living the dream. I was happily married with a great job, a big house, and two kids on the cusp of successful adulthood. My nineteen-year-old daughter, Jess, had recently married the love of her life, and though I'd wished she'd waited until she'd graduated college, I was in awe of the amazing woman she'd become, so full of dreams and hope and promise.

When Jess announced she was pregnant with my first grandson, we all celebrated together at her favorite restaurant. It was a joyful and perfect evening, and none of us would have ever fathomed the possibility that it would be our last night together as a family.

It was just two days later that I got the call. Jess had been in a car accident and "she didn't make it." Hearing those words is like being shot through the heart at close range. Those words are too dangerous to carry; you must dismiss them. The words that say your child is no longer alive cannot possibly register in your brain. A parent cannot let those words be recorded as truth. They're words that tell you that life as you know it will never be the same.

I immediately went into nothingness. It was a box, a compact place, neither light nor dark. It contained no up, no down, no thought, no time, and no space. Everything was happening both in slow motion and at the speed of light. I fell to the floor and screamed. A guttural, animal scream—the kind of scream that can only come from hearing the words that mean your child is dead. My vocabulary was gone. I could only emit a violent, volcanic explosion of every dark emotion. I threw the phone across the room because the phone was a liar. I wanted to destroy that phone; I couldn't throw it hard enough or far enough. My world went black.

As news of the accident spread, our house filled with people. I was in and out of my body, participating and observing. I watched as people came and went and wondered how so many of them could be in agreement about something that could not possibly be true. I went outside to scream. I sobbed uncontrollably. I experienced episodes of insisting I needed to go find my daughter and straighten out the entire situation. No one could meet me where I was. No one could relate to the thoughts running through my mind.

The days and nights that followed were indescribably horrific, and I immediately realized these were cracks I'd never be able to patch. This time, my heart wasn't just broken; it was shattered beyond repair. I sensed a black hole calling to me—a dark, bottomless pit of sorrow that felt abysmally desolate and yet somehow comforting too, a resting place for my agony. One particularly painful evening, my sleeplessness led me to some paper and a pen. I had no idea what I was going to write; I just felt something pushing me to sit in the darkness with these items, as though they somehow held a tiny promise of relief from my relentless suffering.

Words began flying out of my pen. I wasn't thinking the words; they were writing themselves. When the writing stopped, there were two poems that seemed to be messages from Jess. The first was titled "Letters from Heaven," though it did not feel at all like I had been the one to title it. As I sat in my astonishment, reading and rereading the poems, the room filled with an indescribably peaceful feeling. I heard a voice that I instinctively knew was the voice of God. It said, *Look at this hole.* And in that moment, I could see the hole clearly. It was back-lit, though there was no actual source of light in the room.

The voice continued. *The hole is filled with darkness. I know you want to go there, and it's okay if you do. Many parents go in, and everyone will understand if that's what you choose. But if you do go in, I want you to know it could take you a long time to get out, and there is a chance you will never come out at all.* And then the voice was gone, the hole was gone, and I was alone.

I sat there, stunned, wondering if this had actually happened while knowing that it had. I wasn't afraid. I felt empowered. I realized I did not want to go there; I did not want to live in that hole. But what was the alternative? The realization trickled in. To stay out of the hole,

I'd have to take charge of my thoughts. I'd have to consciously turn away from the hole again and again. I'd have to turn my thoughts away from what I had lost and toward what I had gained.

After that miraculous exchange, though I continued to mourn my daughter in every way, I felt the energetic flavor of my mourning shifting. Instead of allowing myself to think, *I'm never going to be able to (insert any activity) with Jess*, I would force myself to think, *What a wonderful nineteen years we had*. Instead of, *I'm never going to have a daughter again*, I'd choose, *I got to be her mom for all those years*.

I began to question everything. What is death? Where do we actually go? If we can still communicate in some form, what does it all mean? Losing Jess broke me open like never before, but I soon realized that those impossible-to-mend cracks had something profound to offer. It was through those very cracks that light began to pour in. Those irreparable cracks were opening the space for my miracles and my most honest growth. I was surrounded by mementos of Jess, from the lock of her hair held by a tiny blue rubber band that I kept in a Ziploc bag in my china cabinet to the charity I started after her death. Yet these reminders no longer brought me grief—only joy and gratitude for her part in my life, and mine in hers.

I started listening to my heart and going where it led. When I felt the nudge to book a trip to see Wayne Dyer speak, I didn't hesitate. I went online and discovered he was presenting at an event in Phoenix that weekend called Celebrate Your Life. I had never heard of the conference or any of the other speakers, but I somehow I just knew I had to go. As my son drove me to the airport, he showed me a logo he had designed for my charity. I'd asked for a heart with a ribbon coming out of it, symbolizing the connection that hearts are able to maintain even after death. That connection was so important to me, and I didn't even realize I was on my way to a conference where many attendees would share that feeling.

It didn't take long for my miracles to start showing up. After enjoying Dyer's keynote presentation, the very first lecture I wandered into was for writers. Thanks to Jess, I'd been taking my writing more seriously and wanted to learn how to hone my craft. Miracle number one occurred after this lecture when I discovered that the presenter, a publisher named Randy Davila, lived in the same tiny Texas town I lived in! (Randy and I went on to become friends, and he introduced me to many of my most cherished teachers, including Byron Katie.)

I was exhausted by Saturday evening, saturated with new knowledge and looking forward to spending some alone time in my room writing, relaxing, and processing. There was a final presentation that night, a keynote, but I didn't even remember who was giving it since I'd never heard the name before. I had no intention of attending the keynote, but as I walked by the conference hall where it was taking place, I again felt that unmistakable nudge.

I peeked inside and was surprised to see a full house of nearly two thousand people waiting for the speaker to arrive. I assumed I'd never get a seat and turned to leave. That was when I noticed a woman near the front of the room gesturing to me. In spite of the fact that I had never seen her before, she was patting an empty seat next to her and motioning for me to take it. When I accepted her invitation, she explained that she'd been saving the seat for a friend who had just let her know she wouldn't be coming. She saw me looking for a seat, so she waved me over. I thanked her and asked, "Who's the speaker?"

"James Van Praagh," she replied.

It was a roller-coaster evening from that moment on. My new friend explained that the speaker was a medium, someone who helped people talk to their deceased loved ones. She was holding a stuffed bear that had belonged to her son, who had died of cancer. A bit of spontaneous eavesdropping clued me in that I was surrounded by parents who had lost children and were there in hopes of getting messages from them.

I want to be clear that at this point in my journey I did not believe in mediums. In spite of my own miraculous connections with Jess, I was convinced that any kind of mediumship that took place on a stage was all smoke and mirrors. Still, I had been intuitively directed to that seat, so I resolved to stay and find out what it was all about.

James Van Praagh appeared and began delivering messages. It all seemed impressive, but I remained skeptical. After about the sixth reading, he began focusing on the row I was sitting in. Once his focus got that close to me, I immediately started feeling a shift in my energy. At first I thought it was just an emotional response to the messages he was giving to others, but then I heard him talking about hair stored in plastic, bound with a small blue rubber band. Before I would consider raising my hand, I asked (in my head), *Jess, is that you?*

From the stage, James said, "And now someone's saying, 'Mom! Mom! It's me!'"

Tentatively, I raised my hand and stood up. One of the mic runners saw me and came over. James looked at me and said, "Ohhh, you're so sweet. I feel like there's a ribbon coming right out of your heart and into mine." I couldn't believe it. He was describing my logo! And he had described the lock of Jess's hair I kept in my china cabinet—right down to the detail of the tiny blue rubber band.

Without me saying a word, he told me my daughter was there, and that she had been a college student killed in a car accident at nineteen. He asked me, "Do the words 'letters from heaven' mean anything to you?"

When I told him it was the title of a poem Jess had written through me after her passing, he said, "Now you're freaking out the psychic guy!" He explained that he was writing a book and *he* had written those very words in the last chapter but didn't know why or what it would turn out to mean. (James later included my poem, "Letters from Heaven," in that chapter of his book.)

I grew up Catholic, and I was not a natural believer in what was happening. I kept trying to figure out how he could know the things he was telling me. A part of me wanted to stay cynical, but the evidence just kept coming.

James told me that Jess was saying she wanted me to follow the advice inscribed in my new ring. Of course he had no way of knowing that I had in my pocket at that very moment a silver ring I had recently purchased for its beautiful interior inscription: "Live by faith, not by sight."

He also said Jess was showing him a paper she'd written—something she was excited about. Before the accident, Jess had written a beautiful paper at college, and after she died, it had been published in a creative writing compilation put out by her school. She was showing it to James so he could let me know that she was aware of this success and was enjoying it.

James asked me if I was a writer, and I quickly said no. He said, "Yeah, you are. You and I are going to be friends for a long time." And now here I am with a chapter in his book and a career writing, speaking, and helping others to hurt less, heal better, and understand the things my devastation has taught me.

Most importantly, what I've learned is this: when life cracks open our hearts in irreparable ways, it is a blessing. Those who work too hard at patching up the cracks will miss out on the magic that's available only to those who make peace with the cracks and learn to live with a truly open heart. The cracks are there to make room for expansion—expansion of knowledge, insight, hope, compassion, and especially love.

Jess's death taught me to live. The cracks in my heart have opened up a life I adore, filled with opportunities I could never have imagined. Before my heart was split wide open, I never had the courage to write, or to be smart, or to be beautiful. Today, a fire has been lit in me that can never be extinguished. I've fallen in love with life, with all people, with God. I've even fallen in love with me. I've made peace with my past and made friends with my future. For the first time in my life, I feel brave. I know I have a job to do, and with each passing day I care less about what anyone thinks about that. I now listen with my heart and see with my mind. Thanks to my miraculous cracks, I am a better person. I do not fear dying, but more importantly, I do not fear living. All of these blessings came as a direct result of my precious daughter's death.

We were not created to live in despair. When the world breaks your heart, leave the cracks alone. Let those cracks provide the openings for darkness to spill out and light to come flowing in. Let the miraculous cracks illuminate your extraordinary path.

꞊ 26 ꞊

Surrender Avenue

Jacob Nordby

From the driver's seat of a U-Haul van, I watched the scorching black snake of highway crawl away across the desert ahead. Swirling dust devils on either side of the road matched the chaos of thoughts that swarmed in my head.

Where am I going?

Why am I doing this?

What will happen when I get there?

That was August 2009, and the road led to Austin, Texas. I was leaving a pile of broken dreams and heartache back in my hometown of Boise, Idaho. A life that once made sense was shattered beyond recognition. The home, reputation, and businesses I had built were all gone—blown away in the financial crisis that had swept across the entire world. All that remained were the few household items we could fit into the small moving truck. My then wife and three young children trailed behind in our car, and I was left alone with my thoughts and the hum of wheels on the road.

What is going to happen to us? I wondered again and again as the miles slid by.

Austin was a town I had visited just once before. I had no friends or contacts, no jobs waiting—nothing but an inner compass needle pointing that direction. Before I left Boise, friends would come over to wish me well and ask, "So, what's in Austin?" I would give them my rehearsed answer with a grin of confidence I did not feel. "I'm going to hit the reset button. You know, write a new chapter in life."

The truth was, I had no idea. I only hoped that my intuition was guiding me into something better than I had left behind. It seemed that way, but the mirage lakes shining up ahead across the highway appeared real, too. Every time I let my mind glance at the uncertainties of our situation, my heart clenched tight in my chest and my stomach churned.

After several days of hard driving, we arrived in Austin, hot, exhausted, and wanting nothing more than home. But this presented a serious problem. Since we had no jobs yet, every rental agent and apartment complex manager told us, "We'd love to help you, but there's nothing we can do until you can prove your income." We were in a strange city, with no solid leads on a place to live. School was about to start for the children, but we could not register them without a permanent address. Our cash reserves could not stand too many days at the extended stay hotel, but no easy solution showed itself. The kids played happily in the pool under the shade of a live oak tree while their mother and I huddled on deck chairs discussing our situation in desperate whispers. Later, eating deli food out of Styrofoam containers, we all watched movies and tried to pretend that everything was normal.

The next day found us in a parking lot in north Austin flipping through rental magazines. Not knowing why or what else to do, I told everyone to buckle up and started driving. The pressure of needing to come up with a solution—and fast—made a knot of fear inside me.

A mile passed on the parkway, and I felt an invisible presence at my shoulder. I don't know who or what it was, but it brought a peaceful suggestion to my mind. *Ask for what you need. You can trust right now. Just let go and let us help you. Surrender.*

Despite my hesitance, I was desperate to find a solution, so I took a deep breath and spoke silently to my Higher Self: *You directed us to this place for reasons I still can't see. I don't have enough light for the path right now, but I surrender to your wisdom and ask for guidance in this moment.*

The next side street off the main road came up on the left, and I felt that I should turn in. Just around the corner was a house that seemed perfect, with a rental sign out front. It was a small brick home with a large tree casting shade on the lawn. The neighborhood was tidy and well kept, built around a sprawling park in the center. The only barrier was our lack of jobs.

I called the out-of-state number on the sign and explained our situation honestly to the landlord. He agreed to work with us, and we moved in the next day. As I pulled the moving truck back into the little side street that led to our new neighborhood, I looked up at the green street sign.

My heart stopped for a beat or two when I saw the name of the road—SURRENDER AVE.

For almost three years, as long as we lived in Austin, I turned on Surrender Avenue every day as I drove to and from work and was reminded that I can trust the wisdom and love of the universe—even when times are frightening.

My situation did not get suddenly easier. The road to healing and stability took its time. I faced the reality of life without all the dreams and plans that had once motivated me. In fact, I was not sure that I would ever recover my basic optimism or stamina that had fueled my previous achievements. One step at a time, I found the gifts and wisdom hidden in those circumstances. A patched together assembly of part-time jobs kept the bills paid and allowed enough space and time to give birth to my long-hidden dream of writing. It was during this time that I wrote most of my first book. Each day, with another forward step of honesty, the path rose to meet my feet in unexpected ways.

I learned to pay attention to the many subtle ways the Universe speaks, dropping clues and hints as It goes. New people and opportunities showed up as guides and teachers to help me find the way home to myself. A little at a time, life emerged from the valley of the shadow of death, and I discovered that surrender is not giving up at all. It is the doorway to true power.

So many years later, after returning to my hometown nestled in the mountains of Idaho, if someone were to ask where the most important lessons of my life were learned, I would have to take out a map and point them to Surrender Avenue, where we once lived in Austin, Texas.

27

Angel in Disguise

Shanda Trofe

There are stretches of interstate in Michigan where you can drive for miles on a forest-lined road and not see a single exit or vehicle in sight. Such was the case as I made the long trek home from my job nearly forty-five minutes away.

I don't recall if it was the late-night shift that had my mind in a daze or if it was the music on the radio that had me lost in my thoughts, but it hadn't occurred to me to check my gas gauge, and lo and behold, along that dark and desolate road, the engine started to sputter.

No, please, this can't be happening. Not now.

It was the middle of winter, and the temperature was below freezing. Fearful thoughts raced through my mind as panic set in. Without a cell phone or a nearby exit, I would be in for a long walk in the snow, with no boots or gloves to protect me from the freezing cold.

Immediately, I asked the angels for help. I cried out in a panic to please let me at least make it to my exit, but that outcome was unlikely, as my car started to slow with miles yet to go. Although the pedal was unresponsive to my unrelenting foot, the pull of the engine miraculously moved me another mile, to the only light on the dark highway, illuminating a closed and deserted truckers' weigh station.

Almost instantaneously, at the very moment my engine died and my car came to a stop, headlights pulled up behind me, as if out of thin air. Mixed emotions washed over me—thrilled that someone could be coming to help me, yet confused as to where they came from, since no one was behind me and hadn't been for the duration of my drive.

With no time to worry about who it could be, I jumped out of my car and ran to the vehicle's side door. The gentleman, who looked to be in his mid-forties, rolled down the window and asked if I needed help. I explained that my car had run out of gas, and he took out his badge, leaning over to show it to me. He was an off-duty police officer willing to help, but first I had to show him my driver's license to prove I was who I claimed to be. I obliged, and in turn he jotted down his name and badge number to confirm his identity.

Thrilled to be rescued, I locked up my car and got into his warm SUV. In retrospect, it may not have been the smartest move to get into a vehicle with a complete stranger in the middle of the night, but considering the circumstances, I didn't have much choice. Plus, there was a feeling of warmth and sincerity about this man, and I instantly trusted him. My intuition told me he was safe, and we chatted briefly as he drove me home. He told me he was on the local police force in my area. Being a small town, we knew several of the same local officers. We chatted about a few of our common acquaintances, and before long I was in my driveway. I assured him I would wake someone up to help me get gas for my car, and he pulled away with a wave. As quickly as he came into my life, he was gone.

I phoned a friend and explained what had happened, and he told me I was crazy to get into a car with a stranger in the middle of the night. He brought over a can of gas and lectured me all the way back to my vehicle as we filled the tank and got my car up and running. Still, not a single other car in sight.

As I settled into the driver's seat once again, gratitude washed over me as I reflected on the events that had transpired. My car had managed to make it to the only streetlight for miles. I was instantly rescued the very moment my car stalled, and I was delivered home safely, without having to walk miles in the freezing winter night.

But where had that SUV come from?

The following day I called up my local police department and asked for my hero by name. I was appreciative of his kind gesture, and I wanted to thank him once again. To my dismay, I was informed there was nobody on the force by that name.

"Hmmm, that's strange. Perhaps I have the name wrong. Here's the badge number."

"Nope, sorry. Nobody on this force by that name."

How could that be? He had told me the name of the force and his sergeant, whom I also knew. We had many of the same acquaintances and chatted about them during the drive. Clearly that badge was real, and he seemed so kind and gentle, he couldn't have been a predator in the night. If he were, he easily could have taken advantage of the situation.

That's when I knew there was only one logical explanation.

It's been said that Archangel Michael is the patron saint of law enforcement. Archangel Michael, meaning "he who is like God," is our loving protector who looks out for us and protects us when called upon. I learned at a young age to call upon the angels when I need help, or for daily protection in general.

As I put the pieces together, it started to make perfect sense. The moment my car started to sputter, I called out to the angels for help. I was miraculously able to drive my car for an additional mile, without gas, until I reached the only streetlight on the long dark stretch of interstate. At the very moment my car shut off, headlights appeared behind my vehicle out of nowhere. An off-duty police officer came to my rescue. A kind stranger delivered me home safely and then disappeared forever, not known by the other officers in the area.

I've never forgotten that night, or the synchronicity of events as they transpired. I've always been one to call upon the angels, but without seeing a physical angel, sometimes we wonder if they are really there, standing by, waiting for us to exercise our free will and allow their loving help and guidance into our lives.

Maybe angels do not always appear as winged entities, as they are often depicted in drawings and folklore. Perhaps angels walk this earth among us each day whose sole purpose is to help those in need. Maybe angels take human form at those times when we call out for assistance. Whatever the case, I'm convinced the angels are always standing by, ready and willing to lovingly help us, protect us, and guide us in our daily lives.

Since this event, I've made it my life's mission to teach others about angels, that they are always there to help and offer guidance whenever we call upon them. The angels can assist in all aspects of our lives, but first we must invite them in to intervene because we have free will.

I've had many miraculous experiences since that cold winter night many years ago. This story in particular serves as a reminder to me that if anyone is ever in a situation where there seems to be no way out, where you're in danger or you just need some divine intervention, you can call upon the angels. Take notice of who shows up to rescue you.

It just may be an angel in disguise.

28

Life After Death

Heidi Connolly

I know what miracles are. I know because I see them happen every day—and because some of them happen to me. I guess you could say I'm proof, or that my life is proof, or, for that matter, that my very existence is proof. There have been so many miracles in my life that choosing just one to write about and calling it the "biggest" would be like loving one of my children more than the other. It's a conundrum I wish on everyone.

I loved my husband, Randy Michael Connolly, until death did us part. So much so that it felt as if I'd died with him. By the time December 2013 rolled around, I'd been praying for my own death for a little over a year, although I still hadn't had the nerve to take my own life and realized I might never find that nerve, no matter how devastated I was. The only thing that could possibly keep me going, as I saw it, was a miracle. I'd need some kind of concrete, measurable evidence that he was still with me, just as he'd promised he'd be before he passed over.

Night after night of crying myself to sleep had mitigated neither my desperation nor my depression. Nor had knowing that there were people around me who were hearing Randy, in spirit form, clearly and irrefutably. Sure, I appreciated the loving messages, as indirect as they were. But what about me? I was his wife, dammit. Didn't I deserve to hear those messages straight from the source?

Finally, one night, a night like all the rest where I'd passed out after hours of tossing and turning and abject anguish (I don't profess to be one of the stoic ones), I was awakened at 3:00 a.m. by a loud voice. This booming voice told me to get out my pen and start writing. Although I can't tell you why, or how, I knew in every cell of my being that this disembodied vocalization belonged to my dead husband. What I did not realize was that the result of this mandate, and the ensuing half hour of notebook scribblings, would be the basis for our first "ghostwritten" book together, *Crossing the Rubicon: Love Poems Past the Point of No Return.*

You might think I'm going to say the miracle was that Randy, in spirit form, woke me up and downloaded a book of poems—along with an almost instant comprehension about how to form a new relationship with your loved one after he or she passes and how to write about it so others might understand and benefit. You might think that the miracle is that since that night I've been able to communicate with Randy, the dead brother of my manicurist, the dead husband of my mother's friend, and many other spirit beings who desire to speak with their loved ones. Either way, you'd be right. But honestly? The most profound and shocking miracle is that without the gift of Randy's dying, I would never have discovered, or perhaps I should say uncovered, the brilliant conscious creation practice that has become my new way of living.

Is it possible to recognize a miracle—a blessing, even—while you feel you're being ripped to shreds? When your soul can't see the proverbial light at the end of the tunnel even if it were wrapped in the glow of every star in the sky? When your heart is gasping for breath in order to survive one more minute, one more hour, one more day? My answer BRD (before Randy's death)? Absolutely not. ARD (after Randy's death)? Absolutely. Even if you're in the throes of agony. Because once your agony has been imbued with conscious awareness, the frequency of unconditional love, the vibration of truth, and the resonance of wisdom, nothing is the same ever again.

For me, on that night, even as I wrote in the dark, sobbing over the pages of an old lined notebook, bleary-eyed from lack of sleep, fear, and the sense that I had been abandoned to fend for myself in a world I could no longer make sense of, I was concomitantly aware that I was feeling a new kind of positivity I had never known before. Even in that state of being completely overwhelmed, I knew I was experiencing something so enormous, so rock-me-to-the-core powerful, that while I couldn't name it at the time, I could feel it blooming inside me, as sure and concrete as the almost invisible scar on the inside of my thigh, the one I'd gotten in a motorcycle mishap in high school. It seemed as if I'd always had this thing that was blooming—always known it, always felt it—but now would never again fail to recognize it or cherish it.

The wave of unconditional love that flowed through me arrived in the form of complete phrases and rhymes, an unabridged conversation. It came in the vibration of truth, through the voice of my dead husband who had always valued integrity above all else. It came in the resonance of wisdom, as a new kind of knowledge I was being invited to believe in, accept, and share. It came with the awareness that even as I wept, and the lead in my pencil dwindled to a stub, I would never be the same again.

And it's true. Nothing *has* ever been the same since that night. I no longer have any need to pretend that I have it all under control, or to pretend that life makes sense. I don't, and it doesn't. This is precisely what makes miracles so . . . miraculous. I now understand that all our attempts to control, fix, cajole, maneuver, manipulate, push, and pray are all simply miracle-*blockers*. When viewed through the lens of retrospection, it's easy to see that miracles are the fruit of faith, not force.

When I met Randy after my first forty years on the planet, I knew *that* was a miracle. The circumstances were too bizarre, too completely without precedent. We agreed that we were two of the truly fortunate ones. We'd prayed for a miracle. We got it. End of story.

Then he died. And I was compelled to ask, what does that say about our supposed miracle? Was I wrong? Were we wrong? Was this a faux miracle? Had I been deceived? If God wanted me to be happy, why take away the one person who made me happy? What kind of an anti-miracle miracle was that? Could something that once looked like a miracle of light and love turn into something dark, something that no longer felt miraculous?

I did not know the answer, but the question itself is what led me deep into realms that I had never previously tapped. I explored karma, life after "death," past lives, and conscious creation. I acquiesced into what has been so aptly called "the dark night of the soul." I allowed myself to be held by those who'd had similar experiences and who encouraged me to believe that I would come out the other side whole again. I eventually learned that my "sensitivity" was simply code for being a medium for the spirit world, and that tapping into that ability would prepare me for becoming a teacher for other sensitives. Finally, ultimately, I learned that miracles are in the eye of the beholder.

The miracle is that I now understand that I contracted with Randy and agreed to be his partner in this lifetime to help him learn that someone (me) could and would love him unconditionally.

The miracle is that Randy is now helping me learn, from the other side of the veil, that having trust and faith in what you can't see is the means by which we can influence the energy that determines everything that happens to us every single day.

The miracle is that I have learned to question every core belief I once held, ever deepening my understanding that the spirit world is always communicating with us, and that it's simply up to us to learn how to listen—and the miracle is that I'm able to share all these insights with others.

The miracle is that I have found love again.

The *biggest miracle* of all, you ask?

That's easy. There is life after death. On *both* sides of the veil.

About the Authors

Thea Alexander

Thea Alexander is a spiritual psychologist, gifted intuitive, spiritual medium, past-life regressionist, and author. Passionate about sharing her experiences and helping others discover the Divine within, an integral part of Dr. Thea's work is bridging the gap between the human condition and spirituality.

Dr. Thea has been experiencing psychic phenomena since early childhood and has spent over twenty years facilitating healing at a soul level by assisting others in developing and deepening their spiritual awareness. Her connection with Spirit communicates with certainty that our soul's journey continues beyond the physical.

Connect with her at www.drtheaalexander.com.

Mandy Berlin

Mandy Berlin, EdM, is an author, teacher, intuitive, and retired scientist. In 1987, she completed her doctoral comprehensive examinations in educational psychology at Arizona State University. Her third book, *Death Is Not "The End": One Agnostic's Journey on the Bumpy Road to Belief*, chronicles Berlin's epiphany following the death of her beloved husband and other loved ones soon after.

The uncanny phenomena she's witnessed firsthand have convinced her that the afterlife awaits us all.

Connect with her at
https://mandyberlin.wordpress.com.

Heidi Connolly

Heidi Connolly incorporates her connection with spirit in everything she does as a writer, editor, self-publishing consultant, musician, and intuitive coach. Her business, Harvard Girl Word & Music Services, offers a unique approach based on many years of developing both her expertise and her intuition. She is the author of several books, including *Crossing the Rubicon* (coauthored with her husband after his death), which incorporates her inspirationally guided, improvisational flute music in the audio version.

She conducts cutting-edge workshops on "ghost-writing" (writing with input from those who have passed on) and writing with conscious intent, hosts the Bandon Afterlife Meetup, and presented a "Dead Ted Talk" at the 2015 Afterlife Awareness Conference. She has been interviewed on the "Dance to Death Afterlife" podcast and Dr. Karen Wyatt's Death Expo 2015. Heidi lives a life of miracles and revelation.

She can be found at www.heidiconnolly.com.

Ellen Cooper

Ellen Cooper, MSW, RN, MSN, is an author and speaker. Currently, she is writing a memoir chronicling her personal experiences growing up adopted, searching for her birth family, and ultimately becoming an adoptive parent herself. She hopes to provide insight into, and a better understanding of, different aspects of adoption while exploring the complex challenges and questions of identity, spirituality, love, and family.

Ellen serves on the board of directors for Adoption Advocates, Inc., an adoption agency in Austin, Texas, and Adoption Knowledge Affiliates, an education and support organization for anyone whose life has been touched by adoption.

Ellen lives in Austin, Texas, with her spouse. She has two children, Hannah and Grant, and one grandson, Camden.

Visit her at: www.ellencooperauthor.com.

Kim Dayoc

Kim Dayoc is a writer, comedian, educator, motivational speaker, and counselor. Having spent most of her teen years homeless, she has seen things many never see and has chosen to find the funny in those situations. Kim has performed on *The View* and has shared the stage with comedy greats such as Carlos Mencia, Ron White, Lewis Black, and many others.

She is working on a book based on her spiritual musings and spends time speaking at school groups and conventions. To read more of her work, visit her blog, The Right Side of 50, at https://kimkerley.wordpress.com.

Laurel Geise

Laurel Geise, MBA, DMin, is a highly sought after international speaker, inspirational author, and business consultant who empowers others to listen, align, and act their way to living their soul's calling. Dr. Laurel is the evolutionary thought leader of the Soul-Guided Living movement and popular host of *Soul-Guided Living*, a weekly radio show featuring experts in the field of personal transformation.

Laurel is the author of multiple inspirational books, including *The Jesus Seeds: Igniting Your Soul-Guided Life*, *The Book of Life: Universal Truths for a New Millennium*, *The New Laws of Spirit*, and *Prophetic Leadership: A Call to Action*.

Laurel travels the world speaking on Soul-Guided Living and consulting with business leaders on Soul-Guided Leadership. when she isn't traveling, she calls St. Petersburg, Florida, home.

Connect with her at www.laurelgeise.com.

Chelsea Hanson

Chelsea Hanson is a nationally recognized grief educator, life and career coach for bereaved women, author of six books, and founder of the online memorial gift and tribute store, With Sympathy Gifts and Keepsakes (www.withsympathygifts.com).

Following the sudden death of both of her parents, Chelsea developed her signature system, the Loss to Legacy Method™, a program that transforms deep grief into insightful healing. Her mission and her calling is leading the bereaved through this unique transformative approach to reconcile their sorrow while continuing to honor the memory of those they love. Her gentle, supportive programs guide survivors on how to live purposefully with new appreciation for each day.

Chelsea's books, grief support programs, and online store have been used by more than 700 funeral homes across the United States and Canada.

Find her at http://chelseahanson.com.

Jodie Harvala

Jodie Harvala is a forward-thinking, spirit-loving, space-clearing psychic teacher and coach. She is also the founder of the Spirit School.

Jodie loves teaching others how to connect fearlessly with Spirit and also how to experience Spirit in the sacred, everyday moments of life. Through the Spirit School, she shares tools and ideas to connect with Spirit on a daily basis and create your own magical experiences. Participants walk away with a fresh perspective regarding the next step on their personal journey here on earth.

To learn more about Jodie and the Spirit School, visit www.jodieharvala.com.

Karen Hasselo

Karen Hasselo, certified spiritual life coach, is the founder of Spirit First Coaching and a facilitator of workshops at the Alive Center in Naperville, Illinois. After Karen's son was diagnosed with autism in 1994, she experienced "the dark night of the soul," which propelled her to master psycho-spiritual healing methods. Her mission is to uplift and empower mothers, ushering special needs children through life. Karen spent sixteen years as a clinical social worker, specializing in adolescents. She received an MA in social work from the University of Chicago and is a graduate of the Holistic Learning Center in New Jersey. Karen is also a contributing author to *No Mistakes!: How You Can Change Adversity into Abundance*. Visit Karen at www.spiritfirstcoaching.com.

Vicki Higgins

As the CEO of Turn Your Stress Into Success and founding partner of the Amazing Over 40® Health Coaching program, Vicki is a certified Life & Health Transformationalist, an international speaker, and a consultant on how to embrace stress and turn it into a catalyst for change. Her neuroscience-based counsel delves into the power of the mind and divine inner spirit to take back control of your health and transform your life.

After twenty years of a successful corporate career in an executive vice president and chief marketing officer role, Vicki felt frustrated and trapped by a vicious, unhealthy stress cycle. So she left and studied with the likes of John Assaraf (her personal mentor) and Dr. Joe Dispenza to discover the amazing secret that busy performance-driven executives are looking for: that stress is only bad for you if you *think* it's bad for you.

A published author in the book *No Mistakes!: How You Can Change Adversity into Abundace*, Vicki has also appeared on television and radio shows and teaches life and health transformation courses online and in live workshops and on stages around the world. She's an adventure junkie and enjoys travel, yoga, hiking, and quality time with friends and family (including her cat, Izzy!).

Visit http://vickihiggins.com to learn more.

Kathy Jackson

It was Kathy's amazing spiritual experience with the passing of her partner's mother, Nola, in 1999 that began a series of conversations and spiritual experiences. Though she had experienced spiritual occurences prior to Nola's passing, it was through this exchange that her life was changed, and Kathy continues to share her experiences with others through her writing, teaching, and coaching.

Kathy is an author, teacher, and intuitive life coach and the founder and Intuitive Visionary of the Spirit-Wind Kidz Ranch in Oklahoma.

Visit www.spiritwindkidzranch.com to learn more.

Karen James

After thirty years of working in the accounting industry, Karen James left her corporate career to pursue her passion for counseling others in grief recovery. She is a certified Grief Recovery Method specialist and teaches groups and individuals. After the death of her daughter, Karen's desire to write was ignited. Her poem, "Letter From Heaven," was featured in James van Praagh's book *Growing Up in Heaven*.

Karen James grew up in Northern California and now resides in Texas. She is the proud mother of two sons and enjoys spending time with her two beautiful grandchildren.

Find out more about Karen and her work at www.kcjames.com.

Sunny Dawn Johnston

Sunny Dawn Johnston is an internationally renowned psychic medium, teacher, author, and motivational speaker.

In December 2003, Sunny founded Sunlight Alliance LLC, a virtual spiritual teaching and healing center. Following her intuitive guidance, she created a place where people can learn how to find and follow their personal spiritual path, recognize and own their natural intuitive gifts, and cultivate a spiritual connection with loved ones who have passed on. Sunny teaches her students that even in moments of adversity we are not alone; our angels, guides, and loved ones who have crossed over are here to help us. Sunny's message that "the love never ends" has drawn thousands of people from all over the world to her workshops, events, and private mediumship sessions.

Sunny is also the best-selling author of *Invoking the Archangels: A Nine-Step Process to Heal Your Body, Mind, and Soul* as well as *No Mistakes, Living Your Purpose, Find Me,* and *The Love Never Ends: Messages from the Other Side.*

Sunny has been featured on many television and radio shows, including "Coast to Coast AM" with George Noory. She has hosted radio shows and recently appeared in the award-winning movie *Sacred Journey of the Heart,* and she was recently seen on Lifetime Movie Network's (LMN) "A Seance with . . ."

To learn more about Sunny's work, see videos, and join her community, visit https://sunnydawnjohnston.com.

Wendy Kitts

At the age of forty-two, Wendy went from a nine-to-five cubicle-gray existence working in accounting to living in Technicolor as a writer—without ever having written anything before. Fifteen years later, Wendy's written three books and over two hundred articles for publications such as *Reader's Digest,* the *Globe and Mail,* and *More* magazine.

Wendy is an Infinite Possibilities certified trainer based on Mike Dooley's *New York Times* best seller *Infinite Possibilities: The Art of Living Your Dreams.* She's following her dreams of living and writing at the beach year-round, splitting her time between Caissie Cape, New Brunswick, Canada, and San Diego, California.

She is passionate about helping fledgling writers share their voices, thereby transforming themselves, their lives, and, by extension, the world. Get your free copy of *Write for Profit & Bliss: Sell Your Writing Now!* at www.wendykitts.ca.

Kristen Marchus-Hemstad

Kristen Marchus-Hemstad grew up in north central North Dakota, the daughter of farming parents. She has a master's degree in counseling and began her career as a crisis counselor. Kristen has always been sensitive, and in 2011, after moving to Texas, she realized her sensitive nature was actually her gift; she was a medium. She has since used her knowledge of Spirit, business, and personal challenges to help her clients through a variety of professional and personal situations.

Kristen is a medium, teacher, mentor, and intuitive counselor providing in-person and phone sessions with clients looking to connect to deceased loved ones, guides, and angels. She also provides classes on a variety of Spirit-related topics.

Kristen lives outside of Austin, Texas, with her husband. Read more about her at www.kristenmarchushemstad.com.

Lisa McCourt

Lisa McCourt is a best-selling author and ghost-blogger specializing in the field of personal transformation. Her joyful passion for the power of words has propelled a diverse publishing career studded with industry awards, starred reviews, international honors, and megasales. On the secret side of Lisa's publishing path, she's ghost-written for many prominent thought leaders, from *New York Times* best-selling authors to Emmy- and Golden

Globe–nominated Hollywood stars. Lisa has also penned over three dozen books in her own name (including the modern classic *I Love You, Stinky Face*) that have together sold over seven million copies. A former popular CBS Radio host and a frequent speaker at both writing conferences and self-growth events, Lisa brings her passion and unique skill set to an eclectic career path that is ever mysteriously unfolding, just the way she likes it.

Meet Lisa at www.lisamccourt.com.

Michelle McDonald Vlastnik

Michelle McDonald Vlastnik is a certified personal trainer, mystic intuitive, and healer with a movement for being authentic and for healing Mother Earth. Her work appears in *365 Days of Angel Prayers*, *365 Ways to Connect with Your Soul*, and *365 Moments of Grace*.

Jessica McKay

Jessica McKay has studied the Toltec spiritual path of wisdom for ten years. Raised in New Jersey, she studied with Allan Hardman, a spiritual teacher in Northern California, with whom she led "Journeys of the Spirit" to Teotihuacán, Mexico, in the Toltec tradition of Miguel Ruiz and *The Four Agreements*. Jessica is a spiritual teacher and intuitive guide, offering clarity and answers to life's questions via intuitive readings at http://intuitivereading.net. She lives with her husband in New Jersey.

Christie Melonson

Dr. Christie Melonson is a licensed psychotherapist and consultant. She is the director of clinical and research services at St. Joseph Children's Home in San Antonio and an adjunct professor of psychology at the University of the Incarnate World. Her professional interests include promoting positive personal and organizational change, advocating for victims of discrimination and abuse, and promoting diversity awareness and equity in organizations. Her writing has been published in professional and self-help genres. Her mission is to make the impossible possible and to help people grow so they can reach their goals.

For more information about Dr. Melonson's services, visit her at http://christiemelonsonlpc.vpweb.com/.

Jean Mulvihill

Jean lives in sunny California near her three kids and two grandchildren. She is currently writing a memoir detailing her experiences parenting a spiritually gifted son.

Connect with her at http://jeanculver.com.

Jacob Nordby

Jacob Nordby is the author of *The Divine Arsonist: A Tale of Awakening* and a contributing author to books with Jack Canfield, Dr. Bernie Siegel, and others. He lives in Boise, Idaho, where he works in publishing, writes books, and coaches aspiring authors on how to tap into their creative genius in his Creative UnBootcamp courses and intensive workshops.

Learn more at http://jacobnordby.com.

Shelly Kay Orr

Shelly Kay Orr is an inspirational teacher, speaker, author, and certified mind-body-spirit practitioner. Shelly's life journey and experience created her unique path to inspire and positively impact others.

In 2012, Shelly received a diagnosis of dissociative identify disorder (DID). The lowest of lows came with an attempted suicide and near-death experience in July 2014. It was in that moment that the noisy, active chorus in her head became laser-focused on the love, unity, and oneness of which all humanity is a part.

Shelly embraced healing and transformed her life from one of merely existing to one of love, hope, and joy. She arrived at a place of clarity and acceptance of her unique gifts and now shares the tools she has learned and developed to help guide others.

After releasing a significant amount of weight through a mind-body-spirit approach, Shelly created an innovative program called *Love Your Body, Feed Your Soul*. This program guides and supports women as they identify and heal the roots of illness and excess weight.

Shelly lives in Oklahoma with her husband and young daughter.

Phoenix Rising Star

Phoenix Rising Star has written numerous articles for magazines including *Awareness Magazine*, *Spirit of Ma'at*, *Heartland Healing*, and *The Edge*. Her books include *The Recipe for Your Soul: 5 Steps to a Delicious Life*, *Ask the Angels: 3 Breakthrough Strategies to Living the Life You Desire*, and *The Confident Launch: Entrepreneurial Success from Conception to Completion*.

Phoenix is an Integrated Energy Therapy (IET®) Master Instructor Trainer, of which there are only twelve in the world. IET is a hands-on therapy that promotes cellular memory healing, and Phoenix has been a Top Master Instructor since 2006. As a trainer and instructor, she travels the United States with her partner Leon, teaching IET classes and offering healing sessions. They call Sedona, Arizona, their home.

Visit http://phoenixrisingstar.com for more information on cellular memory healing and soul path coaching, which Phoenix offers through group and individual sessions.

Janet Rozzi

Janet Rozzi is an author and national speaker who seeks to help people experience intentional living and rediscover their passions. She is proud to be a contributing author of *No Mistakes!: How You Can Change Adversity into Abundance*.

Janet holds a bachelor of science in marketing from Pennsylvania State University and has over twenty years of sales and marketing experience. She lives with her husband in Harrisburg, Pennsylvania. To learn more, visit www.janetrozzi.com.

Deb Snyder

Deb Snyder's exploration into heart-centered living stems from her unique experience with her daughter, Raegan Aria, who was born with a rare brain malformation. Raegan, who is nonverbal, used a form of energy communication to reach out to her intuitive mom during a medical crisis, thus saving her own life. After this amazing experience Deb went on to study the science behind energy, and her mission is to educate and inspire others to shine bright. A board-certified holistic health practitioner, Deb is also the founder and executive director of the HeartGlow Center and the editor of *Inner Tapestry*, a holistic journal in publication in New England for nearly fifteen years.

In addition to her work for *Inner Tapestry*, Deb's articles on spirituality, intuition, telepathy, and parenting have been featured in numerous magazines, websites, newsletters, and publications. She has authored four books, including *Ignite CALM: Bliss at Work*, *The Dogma of Cats for Kids*, *The Dogma of Dogs for Kids*, and *Intuitive Parenting: Listening to the Wisdom of Your Heart*, which won the Gold Mom's Choice and the Silver Nautilus award.

Visit Deb at www.ignitecalm.com.

Marla Steele

Marla Steele is a professional pet psychic and reiki master working with human and animal clients since 2000. She first became aware of her intuitive abilities as a young child through vivid psychic dreams. It wasn't until her late twenties, when she got her first horse, that she entertained the idea of communicating with animals telepathically.

As a voice for animals, Marla reveals their preferences, pinpoints discomfort, negotiates behavior, and reveals how they heal and mirror people. She specializes in delivering messages from pets that have passed on, proving that they are still close by.

Marla has a degree in broadcasting and quips that *now she is the medium*. She has appeared on several radio and TV shows and produced a series of Animal Chakra Dowsing Charts and the Animal Communication Journeys guided meditation CD. She is a contributing author to *365 Days of Angel Prayers*. She teaches others how to talk to, listen to, and heal animals at a soul level through her Access Animal Consciousness training program.

Marla lives in Petaluma, California—yes, a town with "pet" in the name.

Shanda Trofe

Best-selling author, publisher, and writing coach Shanda Trofe is the founder of Spiritual Writers Network, an online community of over three thousand writers and authors, and president and CEO of Transcendent Publishing and Write from the Heart, LLC. Aptly named the "authorpreneur mentor" by her colleagues, Shanda aims to educate aspiring authors not only about the business of writing and publishing but also growing an empire based on the core concepts of their published work.

In addition to working with writers and aspiring authors, Shanda is a certified mind, body, and spirit practitioner, angel therapy practitioner, law of attraction practitioner, and spiritual life coach. She believes that by incorporating spiritual practices into her business she can better serve her clients and lead them toward success.

James Van Praagh

Internationally renowned number-one *New York Times* best-selling author of *Talking to Heaven, Reaching to Heaven, Healing Grief, Heaven and Earth, Looking Beyond, Meditations, Ghosts Among Us, Unfinished Business, Growing Up in Heaven,* and, most recently, *Adventures of the Soul,* James Van Praagh is hailed throughout the world as the pioneer of the mediumship movement and recognized as one of the most accurate spiritual mediums working today. His messages have brought solace, peace, and spiritual insights, changing millions' views of life and death. He has received many awards for his dedication to raising the consciousness of the planet.

James has appeared on virtually every national radio and television show, including *Oprah, Larry King Live, Dr. Phil, 48 Hours, The View, The Joy Behar Show, Chelsea*

Lately, Coast to Coast AM, and many more. He was the creator and executive producer of CBS's long-running series *The Ghost Whisperer*, starring Jennifer Love Hewitt.

James can currently be heard on his weekly Hay House radio show. He stays in touch with fans through his website and blog at www.vanpraagh.com and via social media.

books that inspire your body, mind, and spirit

Hierophant Publishing
8301 Broadway, Suite 219
San Antonio, TX 78209
888-800-4240

www.hierophantpublishing.com